The Isle of the Dragon

The Last Flight of the Bugs Bunny

by Rolf Stibbe

With Best Regards,
Rolf S. Stibbe.
15. March 2020.

Mit Freundlichen Grüßen!

DORRANCE
PUBLISHING CO
EST. 1920
PITTSBURGH, PENNSYLVANIA 15238

(with Freindly regards)

Dorrance Publishing Co
585 Alpha Drive
Pittsburgh, PA 15238
Visit our website at www.dorrancebookstore.com

ISBN: 978-1-4809-9503-1
eISBN: 978-1-4809-9576-5

"Fighting the United States is like fighting the whole world…Tokyo will be burnt to the ground three times."

Japanese Admiral Isoroku Yamamoto, Architect of December 7, 1941 attack on Pearl Harbor, Hawaii

Acknowledgement

The author would like to thank the following individuals and institutions for their gracious support in making the publication of this book possible. Jennifer Holle, Jörg Homburg for their kind assistance for editing the manuscript. The photographic research was completed through the efforts of LTC (Ret.) Jim Pool and vintage aviation historian Carole Gumm, and the extensive photographic collections of Deutsche Bundesarchiv, Germany. www.bild.bundesarchiv.de and World War II Database ww2db.com. are to be commended as well. Extra thanks for additional historical material from Model Art Australia, based in Ringwood, Australia . I offer my sincerest thanks to the late LTC (Ret.) Erwin Werhand and beloved wife Olive Werhand for sharing their vast experiences and war photo collection with me.

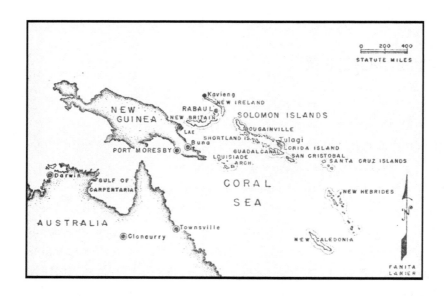

The Theater of Operations of the 823rd 'Tigers' Bomb Squadron in the South Pacific 1943.

(Image from The Army Air Forces in World War II, Volume IV - The Pacific: Guadalcanal to Saipan, August 1942 to July 1944, edited by W.E. Craven & J.L. Cate, at page 5.)

ON AUGUST 19, 1943, the 823rd Bomb Squadron The "Tigers," based in New Guinea, undertook a daring raid against a heavily defended 'Tokyo Express' convoy of reinforcements en route to the island of Bougainville. Admiral William 'Bull' Halsey, commander of the Allied naval forces in the southwest Pacific, hoped that such an air strike by this unit and others would render a strategic blow to the navy of Imperial Japan in the Solomon Islands. The brave men of the United States Army Air Corps were faced with the ultimate challenge once again. For one such B-25 Mitchell bomber participating in the raid, proudly sporting its Warner Brothers *Bugs Bunny* cartoon character nose art on the side, it was to become a truly unforgettable flight.

THEY HAD A MISSION...TO SURVIVE...

With the early morning sunrise over the territory of New Guinea, we find a young American Associated Press newspaper reporter from New York City, Jerry Argendizo, sitting on a hill overlooking the tropical rainforest. All is quiet. The reporter lights his cigarette and begins to write a letter to his mother.

> *Dear Mom:*
> *August 19,1943*
>
> *A new day arrives with the rising sun. It is hot and sticky as hell, we are constantly battling the swarms of mosquitoes in the jungle of New Guinea.*

(The newsman curses, swings his notepad, and kills one of them that had been resting on his left thigh. He grimaces slightly over the blood stain left on his letter and continues writing.)

> *We got big ones down here; see for yourself...sorry for the mess! The aircrews I've been covering this month are doing okay but haven't had a break in weeks. Their nerves are wearing thin*

and they scratch each other's eyes out like tigers before air combat. Those Japanese are really keeping us on the ball. The bets are climbing in the "Beer Shack" that one aircrew will be on top with the most successful missions flown. Our bombers run on plenty of liquid courage these days. There isn't enough time to be afraid as the Japs try to bring down our "Castle in the Sky" every day. We have lost a few guys, but warm bodies just keep coming in from the States to fill the slots. My number hasn't come up at the deli yet. Better not! I have flown with one crew on a few missions. Captain Ed Layton, our "Top Dog," will keep us safe. I am doing an editorial spotlight on him and his crew. Remember, I told you about him in my last letter.

The pilot, Captain Ed Layton, is from Waupaca, Wisconsin, and he's the best B-25 Mitchell pilot I've ever interviewed. Several times they've lost an engine and Ed has always managed to bring them home without becoming shark bait. He plays the cockpit trim wheel like a roulette wheel and gambles that he'll win. There isn't anything that can bring us down, not with him in the cockpit. I now have a chance to go on more missions with him to see more intense combat that scares the crap out of me.

Then there's Lieutenant Randy "Tex" Foster, the copilot, tall and built like a cornstalk. Thinks he's a good card player... I sweep that cowboy every time. He calls me a "Carpetbagger." I will tell you Mom that he's very strong. Sometimes I thought we were goners, but he was always there to pull us through. Tex and the captain are the best wrestling tag team combination. The lieutenant is down to earth and there is a story behind the pilot wings he wears on his chest. I am sure I will hear it someday. The badge seems to be quite precious to him.

Sergeant Daryl Ford, the bomber top turret gunner, nicknamed 'Injun Joe,' is a rather quiet fellow. I've flown with him twice and I still haven't figured him out. You should see some *of his tribal woodcarvings, a sure-fire millionaire at any rummage or craft sale back in the States that's for sure.*

And of course who can forget George Komorowski, the big Kielbasa from Chicago? I've never seen a guy closer to God than him. I can't blame him though from what he's experienced so far. I'm just as scared and nervous as he is. He prays a lot, even though I don't understand Polish. The power of prayer doesn't need words. I wear my St. Christopher's Medal everyday as added protection against the enemy bullets. I carry it right over my heart. Why? This unit has lost a bunch of guys—a bunch of buddies...brothers in arms. There are so many new faces coming in it isn't funny.

Speaking of replacements, Layton's crew got a new tail gunner last week, Tech Sergeant 'Chuck' Wozniak from Cleveland, to replace a guy who bought the farm after taking a bullet in the head. He's a good artist and likes to tell wild stories. I do feel safe with him guarding our plane's tail. He handles the fifty caliber machine guns like a professional.

I finally got your letter. It took forever to get here from Brooklyn. Are you sure the mail ships aren't circling around Ellis Island? Lady Liberty would be quite angry knowing that her boys are not getting their mail from home before they died in this jungle or at sea. I just want you to know that all is well and I have so much news material to sift through it isn't funny. The missions just keep on coming, hopefully we'll come back. I just wanted to say that I love you and will write again soon. Your Bambino.

P.S. A big hungry rat ate the last of the cookies you sent. Could you please whip up another batch for me? Grazie! There is one thing I want to know... after this war is over, was it all worth it?

The press agent leaves and returns to the airfield.

The Mission Briefing

The daring 'Tiger' aircrews were determined to put out the light of Imperial Japan's Rising Sun. They woke up and had breakfast on their small airstrip in Port Moresby, New Guinea. This crack unit within the 38th Bombardment Group prepared itself for another mission against Japanese shipping. In the mess tent, word had been silently passed that their up-and-coming deployment to another airfield had been put on hold. Confusion spread through the ranks as they were informed of an emergency briefing in half an hour. The pilots and their copilots quickly downed their breakfast and hustled over to the flight operations tent to make some sense of the confusion. Once inside the briefing area, they descended on the rough benches and began to talk between themselves, with topics relating to mail from home, baseball scores, and their last mission. One lieutenant leans over to his copilot and says, "I heard that the movie *Heaven Can Wait* just hit the pictures back in the States. Boy I'd sure like to be in Don Ameche's shoes. I'm not in a hurry to get my angel's wings." Captain Layton and copilot Lieutenant Foster enter and join the others on the benches. In front of them is a large map of New Guinea and the Solomon Islands. It is another steamy morning. A sergeant enters the tent and faces the group. He calls the men to attention. The pilots stop talking and snap to attention as their squadron commander enters the tent, followed by his aide carrying a map case. With them are weather and intelligence men. Colonel Ryan Kendall, the 823rd's rugged commander, then orders his men at ease, to which they return to their seats. Colonel Kendall addresses his pilots:

"Good morning men. Before I get started this morning, our wing commander and I would like to congratulate you all for the mission flown on Monday. Job well done. Your raid in the Bismark Sea caught the Japs completely by surprise. We sent nine ships to the bottom, including three tankers. This should cripple the Japanese sortie rate for the next week." The tent fills with the sounds of applause and cheering. "We know that you guys are very keen on finding your targets...but some of us *still* need help with landing. Lieutenant Cunningham for example (the other pilots snicker), saw fit to bring his ship down in the middle of a sugar cane field." The pilots burst out in laughter. Cunningham is obviously embarrassed and gets patted on the shoulder by comrades. "It took crash and recovery a whole day just to get that thing out of the mud, let alone settle down the farmer!" The laughter continued. "Cunningham, the plane arrives on base today. You can help pull it off the trailer and put it back together again. Guys, you got maps...Damn it, use them!" The snickering subsides in the tent with the start of the briefing.

"You are probably wondering why I called you in here this early. I didn't get much sleep myself and thought we'd get a day off. The phone from HQ rang off the hook. We have to give some other groups a hand since we're short of planes again. We will not be flying northward toward the Dutch East Indies, but east towards Rabaul." The airmen quietly speak among themselves with apprehension. This harbor strikes fear into the heart of every Allied aviator. Rabaul is a stronghold harboring some of Japan's best combat fighter squadrons and formidable naval fleet installations, with lots of anti-aircraft guns.

"The situation is becoming critical gentlemen, let me get right to the point." The colonel grabs his pointer and steps up to the large map of the Solomon Islands. "As you know, our guys landed on Vella Lavella and took it on the 15th by passing Kolombangara, which is packed with Japanese soldiers. Let them starve. Admiral Halsey wants to invade and establish airfields on Bougainville and use them as a springboard to hit Rabaul on New Britain. He wants to change the name of Rabaul to Rubble." Not a sound is heard as fear envelops the entire tent.

"G-2 intelligence and coast watchers were monitoring Japanese radio and code traffic late yesterday and are convinced that Admiral Mineichi Koga's Third Fleet intends to send another 'Tokyo Express' convoy of reinforcements to Bougainville today. Right here (points at the map) at Empress Augusta Bay. Aerial reconnaissance planes confirm this buildup of forces in Rabaul. Men, we have to stop this convoy. Admiral Nimitz's ground troops are depending on us to get the job done. For every troop transport we sink, it's one less soldier they will have to face in that God-forsaken jungle of Bougainville. To make things worse, intelligence also tells us that Koga has decided to pull some of his top-notch pilots off his carrier decks and station them on Rabaul." The men react with whispering voices of fear. Kendall tries to reassure his men.

"Guys, settle down…Hey…our Fifth Air Force tacticians devised an attack plan last night, called Operation SQUEEZE PLAY. Four squadrons of bombers are to meet the 'Tokyo Express' right here (points at the map), south of Rabaul, and plaster them with bombs this afternoon. Then, get the hell out before the land-based fighters on Rabaul and Bougainville have a chance to react. Our planners believe that we have a good chance to do some damage to *Tojo* (Japanese Warlord General *Hideki Tojo*) in this area. There will be no secondary target… no group steps down for maintenance. This will be a maximum effort gentlemen, we will have runners on first, second, and third, and we've got to score. Today we're going to win big."

"The raid will consist of roughly forty aircraft divided into groups that will hit the convoy in four waves. We will be in the last group. We pull the wheel chocks at noon, group, and then head for the target. There is also a bit of urgency in this whole affair, as our weather boys will soon point out…So listen up."

Master Sergeant Bob Wilson then steps forward, opens his map case, shuffles a few papers, and begins his presentation. "Men, I've got some good news and bad news for you."

"What's the good news Bob?" shouts the aircrews in unison with slight humor.

"As of today I can promise you good weather and visibility over the target area. The northeast trade winds off the Solomons will be roughly twenty knots, a light head wind, and then increasing to roughly thirty-five knots in the afternoon. This should give you a good tail wind to push you out of the area."

A pilot in the crowd then calls out, "What's the bad news?" The smile disappears from Wilson's face.

"I would like you to know that we have a bit of rough weather, a typhoon, heading towards the Solomons. We thought that the system would veer off, but it didn't, and there is no telling exactly where it is headed. Heck I don't know. The timing of this strike is critical. I don't think that the weather will give you serious trouble; maybe you'll just catch the edge of the storm. You know as well as I do that the weather conditions in this area of the Pacific can change rapidly. We are keeping our eyes on this situation. One thing we know is that the air pressures near Bougainville are dropping a bit." The briefing tent is once again dead silent as Wilson points out the island of Bougainville on the map with a pointer. "If, and I say if, the weather continues to deteriorate, then believe me, we will scrub the mission." There is a slight sigh among the aircrew. They loosen up a bit. "Once you have finished with your runs, get out right away. That is all I have Colonel."

Squadron Commander Kendall interrupts: "Admiral Spruance has suspended all flight operations until the storm damage assessment of his fleet from that typhoon is finished. His attack on the Gilberts has been postponed. It is crucial that we hit this convoy and as Sergeant Wilson just told you, get out fast. I'm sure that the Japanese won't expect our arrival due to the weather situation, probably even using it as cover for their landing force. I'll bet we give them a nasty surprise as they sail right under our bombs."

"Oh, before I forget, I also have a message from our sister group. Just came off the wire. It seems that they ran into a real hornets nest of Zeros off Lae yesterday, losing six bombers. Captain Robert Thompson was among them. He was a top-notch pilot with fifty-one successful missions, and a damn good ping-pong player at last year's inter-service championship. You can read his obituary in tomorrow's *Stars and Stripes*. Let's do this one for ole Rob. This leaves Captain Layton, our

"Captain of the Clouds," on top with forty-two successful missions completed." The pilots in the room begin their respectful applause. Layton sits quietly, unmoved.

"Don't let victory go to your heads men...The war in the Pacific is far from over, just stay sharp and fly like we trained you. The pilots of the Army Air Corps are the best trained in the world, and don't you forget that. If there aren't any questions, the individual group briefings will begin at 1100 hours, and maintenance is getting our planes ready for this mission. They tell me a fresh supply of oil filters and magnetos have just arrived from the States. See you on the flight line. We pull chocks at noon." The commander begins to walk away as the room is again called to attention. After he steps outside, the sergeant yells out "At ease!" The intelligence officer then appears to begin the evaluation of Japanese defenses to be encountered. He starts the briefing.

"All right men, listen up. We want to make you aware of some threats that you will be up against in the Rabaul combat area. Now, there is a new Japanese Zero fighter, now code-named the 'Hamp' with the pushing and shoving of General 'Hap' Arnold. This new A6M3 Type 22 has a noticeable change in wing design, which has been shortened. This gives the plane a more nimble, crisp performance in the air. You have seen the older A6M2 Zero in combat, used since the Japs hit us in Hawaii. Our technical department believes that the plane may have a turbocharger, with an increase in performance, and possible addition of self-sealing fuel tanks. So when you hit them, they won't turn into a big ball of fire so easily." Laughter engulfs the tent. "Keep a sharp lookout for these new planes, and regardless of the name change, the fighter is still armed with the same dangerous 20 millimeter cannons. Remember, the difference is in the wing design." The men study the new technical drawing, which is now placed on the easel in front of them. The captain continues his briefing.

"There is also a Japanese destroyer that you will no doubt be seeing on this mission. The ship is of the *Fubuki* class, with an estimated top speed of over thirty-five knots. It can be identified by its distinctive design, as shown here." A corporal then sets up the large sketch of the destroyer on the second easel for all to see. "Note the increase in anti-aircraft guns on the deck, of 25 millimeter and 13 millimeter caliber. These nasty things will be guarding the flanks of the Bougainville assault force. Avoid if at all possible."

The Flight Line

Layton and Tex exit the briefing and begin their walk to the flight line. As they pass a B-25 named *Ace of Spades,* a mechanic whose head is protruding from the cockpit window, busily polishing the windscreen, remarks, "Hey Captain, did you hear about Thompson going down?" "Yup," Layton replies.

"I'll be carrying my lucky rabbit's foot (pulls it out from his uniform) for you on this next one," the crewman says with a smile.

"That's comforting to know. I'll be sure to remember that." Layton snaps back. Lieutenant Foster then enters the conversation with some humor.

"Boy we got one hell of a bunch of confident guys... Maybe we should take Rocco the squadron pig on our plane; he can sit in my seat. I'll stay back here and do all the flight paperwork."

"No," Layton replies, "I'm going to need your help getting us back here because I know we made mistakes from time to time. Remember what happened last month, we had a tough mission and you directed us to the wrong airfield, landing at that Marine Black Sheep Squadron corsair unit. Some of those grunts put George and Daryl in the hospital after a fight in the mess hall." Both men chuckle as they walk through the parked planes.

"Don't worry Sir, it won't happen again." Foster comments.

Layton reaches into his pants pocket and unfolds a slip of paper. "All right, let's see whose bird we'll have today." He studies the handwritten note and remarks, "Hopefully not the *Las Vegas Avenger*. That plane's hydraulic system is finished... it's more like a flying coffin. Hmmm... *Bugs Bunny*, never heard of this one, must be a new one from the States. There it is, on the right, the one that they are painting the Tiger emblem on its nose. Let's go check her out."

The pilot and copilot greet their trusty crew chief Frank Johnson. Lieutenant Foster shakes Frank's hand. "Where is she from? The new planes keep coming, but the pilots are always missing from the bill of sale."

The crew chief adjusts his hat and remarks, "We got her three days ago from our sister group. We're one plane short. Remember, Cunningham wrecked one so they gave us this bucket of bolts. A guy who delivered it yesterday took some hits just aft of the waist. Captain, stick out your hand." The captain extends his right hand. The sergeant places the mangled remains of bullets in his hand. "Boy those Japs use some pretty wicked stuff." He then holds a mangled bullet up before the pilot. "I wouldn't fly in this crate without a helmet and sitting on a flak vest, I'm telling you. These bullets cut through the aircraft skin like butter. I was at Pearl and had to fix the holes in the new B-17's that came in from California on the 7th. He pats the fuselage and remarks "Sorry *Bugs*, on this island it's bailing wire and beer cans I'm afraid. Any word yet from the brass as to when we're shipping out?" The pilot answers that the move had been postponed while the copilot enters the crew hatch and heads for the cockpit to check out the new arrival.

Layton and Johnson walk toward the left wing of the bomber as a mechanic drains a small quantity of gas from a wing tank to remove any accumulated water. The corporal then hands a clear glass of drained fuel to the chief. The sergeant shows Layton the glass. "See this...It's water... If left in the tank it starts to grow nasty green slime and messes up the carbs and fuel lines. Then you can't get away from the Zeros as fast as you'd like to...I don't trust planes borrowed from other groups, so I gave this one a good inspection. "Here's the scoop on what we done to it so far." He references the logbook. "Tires...oil and filters changed on one and two (engines), fresh 'mags (magnetos) on both of them, and the flight controls have been re-rigged...snugged up a bit. There are a few things left to be done, nothing too serious." The captain signs off the completed work in the aircraft logbook, thanks his crew chief and turns to walk away. The crew chief interrupts for the last time, "Oh, before I forget Captain, there won't be time to get the compass swung. We'll get it on Thursday. It is overdue, according to the flight hours. If you guys fly off and get lost, make sure it's Australia. Get me some beer Sir, I could use it in this God-forsaken heat. The lieutenant up there (pointing to the cockpit) can arrange that." The crew chief departs.

Layton climbs aboard *Bugs Bunny* with the logbook as he checks some equipment in the aft fuselage for security of attachment, tightening down several harnesses along the way. Randy sits in his copilot's seat and begins singing his own lyrics to a popular Bob Hope song. "Thanks for the memories, the Zeros off Rabaul, the flak that scared us all, one engine's out, we're bailing out..." and is then quickly interrupted by the appearance of his boss and promptly stops singing. Layton meets the flustered copilot as he looks out the cockpit side window and yells "Clear!" ensuring the flight surfaces are free of obstruction. Ed tosses the logbook into the pilot's seat. Foster cycles the control column and rudder pedals, checking for freedom of movement. A smile appears on his face as he remarks, "We got one nice Mitchell today... good and tight." The pilot squats in the doorway to the cockpit and views his trusty copilot pre-flighting his bird.

"Any word from home yet?" Foster asks. "How's your dungaree doll and the new arrival?" "Everything with Laura is going well so far. The in-laws are excited to see their new little girl, my little pumpkin," Layton says with a smile after removing his flight cap. "I miss them." He reaches into his flight jacket and pulls out a picture of the newborn and hands it to the Texan. "Very nice… What a sweet little angel." Foster returns the photo to Layton. "What's her name?" "Ann Marie Layton," the proud father replies. Captain Layton then asks his copilot about his entrance into military aviation. "What made you want to join the Army Air Corps and get into this mess, Lieutenant?"

"Well," the copilot replies. "Back in Abilene I saw pilots barnstorming in those old Curtis Jennies. It looked like a lot of fun twisting and turning above the farm fields. My parents thought I was crazy for joining, and I am, you know (makes a crazy face). That's why I'm sitting here with you."

"After Pearl Harbor I enlisted and graduated from flight school at Kelly Airfield in San Antonio. Graduating was a great feeling for me. I remember we were all standing at attention as our squadron commander gave us a farewell address before pinning our wings on. He told us,

'When you get your wings, you're going to get a bag of luck. When the bag of luck runs out…then you better watch out.' He then came and pinned the wings on me and said 'Son, here's your bag of luck. Use it sparingly.' I joined the 823rd in Savannah before Easter and arrived here. That's my story Ed. What about you? How did you get here?"

"Early last year I was flying a B-26 Marauder in a training flight, and I felt like a king. I had conquered the plane that killed a lot of our guys. 'A Marauder a day in Tampa Bay,' they said. Heck, it didn't make *my* wife a widow, that's for sure. Anyway, one day I was upstairs flying and the tower called up to me and said, 'Stay up for another fifteen to twenty minutes.' I then thought, 'Wait a minute! What's going on?' So I stayed up. When I landed, they said 'You've got enough flying time now…Pack your bags, you're going overseas.' I was sent to Midway in the '26 and assigned to the 69th Bomb Squadron. Man, those Zeros tore us apart there! They told us to hit the Japs with torpedoes jerry-rigged under our wings and prove that Mad-Man Mitchell was right again. (Mad-Man Mitchell was Brigadier General "Billy" Mitchell, an early proponent of airpower against ships). Planes can sink ships. Out of the four of us, only two ever made it back. My plane was written off. After Guadalcanal, I took leave back to the States and was transferred to Greenville, South Carolina to learn to fly this thing. She's not a bad plane." He then taps the aircraft's metal structure.

The aircrews get into their flight gear and mentally prepare for the afternoon mission. They leave their tents and head for the flight line. The sounds of Bob Hope and his latest USO tour of the Pacific are heard over the base loudspeakers. In the weather tent, the weathermen are busy, and Sergeant Wilson is among them, analyzing new dispatches from ships and planes in the vicinity of the Solomon Islands.

Corporal Berger monitors radio traffic to include atmospheric data with his headset on. He scribbles the latest weather observations on his notepad and signs off the radio. The teenager from Sacramento, California then stands up to confront his supervisor on some startling information. "Sergeant Wilson, Sir!"

"What is it?" replied the senior sergeant.

"I have received some of the latest dispatches from ships in the area, Sir. Take a look at this." He hands the meteorologist his notepad.

Wilson reads aloud: "Freighter *Antonov Petrovich* at 3 degrees south, 167 degrees East longitude, and tanker *Acropolis* at 1-degree north, 159 degrees east longitude, reports air pressures of 990mb, wind 40 knots, with 20-foot swells.

The corporal interrupts, "We even intercepted a report from a Jap freighter, the *Kobyashi Maru*, at 2 degrees south and 174 degrees east, reporting 980 mb, 45-knot wind gusts, and almost 30-foot waves."

There is silence in the room as Sergeant Bob Wilson then places wooden chips on the large map on the table before him, plotting the relative positions of the vessels. He then reaches for his coffee, takes a nervous sip, and remarks, "This doesn't look good. I knew it, I knew it!"

Berger looks at his colleagues and utters a word striking fear into everyone's hearts. "Typhoon." Wilson wipes the sweat off his brow in the warm humid air and assesses the situation while once again staring at the large map table before him. The situation is now critical, as it appears that Colonel Kendall may lead the last leg of the strike force into the path of a dangerous storm. "Admiral Halsey's ships got battered last week by that thing, and now this… heading for the target area. Corporal Berger, get me Colonel Kendall please." The young soldier then leaves the weather tent with great haste.

The airman walks in a brisk pace across the small airstrip and arrives at the tent of the squadron commander. He pauses with fear in front of the simple wooden door, crudely labeled "Kendall," and manages a weak knock. There is no answer. He then builds his resolve and knocks once again with a bit of force. "What is it?!" barks the colonel. The corporal is quite nervous and shouts out "Colonel Kendall, Sir! You need to get to the weather tent right away Sir! Urgent!"

There is silence. "Tell Sergeant Wilson that I am coming... all right!" Kendall replies with irritation.

Berger acknowledges the officer and then quickly scampers off and returns to his post.

Within minutes, the half-dressed squadron commander appears in the weather tent, irritated as usual. Kendall is highly optimistic on dealing another punch into any Japanese effort to support their beleaguered forces marooned on Bougainville. He has little time for anything to distract or impede his path to victory against the infamous foe. The colonel had lost a brother, a gunnery officer, serving on the battleship Oklahoma, which capsized at Pearl Harbor two years previously. "You have news for me Bob?" as he faces the meteorologist with a stern look on his face. Sergeant Wilson answers, "Sir, sorry to break the news to you, but, the weather has taken a turn for the worse...You may have to cancel the mission." The colonel exchanges a grin amongst the frightened staff in the tent. Wilson will not back down. "I am not joking Colonel, look here on this map table." The men congregate around it, with the meteorologist holding the notepad of radio data. "Sir, we have received information about falling air pressures, high winds, rain, and large waves. What we are looking at here, is a large storm, more than likely a big typhoon, a strong one, heading right to where you will be flying...and."

The colonel abruptly cuts off the sergeant's sentence. "I will take your *guess* into consideration before I file my flight plan with my navigator, okay?" The personnel in the room are simply confused at the hasty remark and exchange silent looks of sheer disbelief. In the wake of all the evidence of the approach of a severe storm, their efforts will come to naught.

The meteorologist confronts the commander yet again, "A guess! Sir, these conclusions are based on confirmed radio reports from our ships, and even enemy merchant traffic." Corporal Berger is about to faint in the stifling atmosphere. "Sir... Ryan" now addressing the colonel by first name, in a last act of desperation. "That storm will most certainly give you trouble. Please, contact the air group commander, HQ, call off this raid!"

"Can't do that soldier, we have reports that three large troopships, and freighters overloaded with tanks and guns, will be landing at Empress Augusta Bay later this afternoon. Come rain or come shine, we gotta sink those Jap ships."

Corporal Berger quietly interjects, 'Sir, it's a typhoon...Remember what happened to Admiral Halsey's fleet...quite a few ships, disappeared. Let the storm finish off the 'Tokyo Express'!"

The colonel wipes the sweat from his head, stares down the occupants of the tent, and remarks, "I'm sorry gentleman, the mission will go on as planned. Is there anything else?"

Not a sound is heard. "I thought not," and the officer heads for the door. He pauses briefly and addresses the men for the last time. "Trust me, I know what I am doing..." He exits. Berger then approaches Sergeant Wilson and remarks, "Should we tell the pilots about the latest storm track?"

The meteorologist nods his head signaling "Yes, I will do it, and all you guys keep quiet!" The young soldier then breathes a sigh of relief. "I hope you don't get caught. Kendall will have you strung up if he finds out." Sergeant Wilson chuckles to himself and then leaves the tent.

Takeoff!

As the clock hands strike 11:00, the flight line is full of activity as fuel trucks scramble among the aircraft dispensing the precious fluid. Layton's crew gathers around *Bugs Bunny* as the captain begins his pre-flight briefing. "All right guys, in a few minutes we've got a big one. The mission is 'SQUEEZE PLAY.'" Ed unfolds his tired map. "There are four squadrons of B-25's in today's mission to hit a Jap convoy of reinforcements heading for Bougainville. They are carrying troops, tanks—the whole smash. We're in on this raid, coming in low in the *last* group at the back of the bus."

The crew breathes a sigh of relief as George Komorowski remarks, "Thank God, we always had to go first! But Christ! Why at mast height? A Jap on the ship's deck could hit us with a monkey wrench!" Foster then interjects with a smile, while adjusting his sunglasses and balancing on the gunner's shoulder, "George, you know they always save the best for last, and that's us! We will be coming in so low that you will be able to see them crapping in their Samurai shorts when they see that five hundred pound bomb coming right over their heads!" The laughter is contagious and well deserved before they board *Bugs Bunny* on a flight path to almost certain death. Layton continues, "The trouble is that the weather is going to be rough with the typhoon you heard about. Kendall kept it hush-hush, but thanks to Bob, news of the storm is all over this base, in the beer shack, chow hall, and latrines. He cornered me about ten minutes ago and was nervous as hell." Layton runs his pencil along the map and continues the discussion. "Headquarters has told us that we have to send 'em to the bottom before they reach Empress Augusta Bay; otherwise a lot of our footsloggers (slang for combat infantryman) will get clobbered when they land on Bougainville. I know that we're on top with forty-two missions, and the bets are climbing in the shack. I'll make sure that we'll get some leave soon. We haven't had any in a long time and some of you guys are at the end of your tether. Let's synch our watches. At my mark it will be 1135. This is going to be a long mission, hit the latrine again if you need to. Let's make it a good one! Lieutenant, here's the flight plan."

"Lieutenant Sir, can you see to it that we get off course and land in Australia?" remarks Daryl, the top turret gunner. "I wanna see Australia and all those women and drink the beer!" The crew whistles in unison with delight. Layton could not agree with them more and states, "Sergeant when this is over, I will get you that paperwork, so you can go down there and see the kangaroos. I heard that we may be getting a unit citation after this raid, and is entered into the war journal for the week. Stay sharp and keep your eyes wide open. We will have no fighter escort on this mission. Conserve your ammo and fire in short bursts only. You know the drill guys.

Wozniak, our new set of boots, if you have any questions on the way over, just ring me up on the interphone. Got it?" The Cleveland-area native nods his head in agreement.

George then asks his pilot, "Hey 'Cap, what's with the Press?" (pointing to the A.P. man) "Why is he coming along again? Gonna drop copies of the Associated Press on the Japanese? I think it's just too dangerous."

Argendizo takes slight offense with the remark and lets it be known, "Hey, no wait just a minute fellas! I'm not here to recruit you for a war bond drive!"

Tail gunner Wozniak jumps right in with justified criticism, "That's right Sergeant Komorowoski, with him aboard it's one less bomb to carry." A verbal scuffle ensues as the newsman tries to restore order, setting the record straight.

"George, guys, don't worry. I'm going back to Manhattan at the end of next week. I'm coming up with you to finish off my news article. You guys will be front page news back home. Just think of it."

Daryl strikes upon a great idea and places his hand on Jerry's shoulder, "If you can guarantee putting us all on a *Hollywood* war bond drive, with Hedy Lamarr *and* Rita Hayworth, heck you can fly with me any day!" Laughter once again erupts but is disrupted by the sound of an aircraft engine starting. Layton marshals his men to the aircraft.

"All right, mount up guys! Here we go!" The men walk towards the *Bugs Bunny* as George gets the last word in, as usual. "Jerry, ever fire a 50-caliber machine gun?"

"Nope!" the press agent replies.

"Good, you just met the Air Corps requirements; I'll teach you a bit of fancy shooting when we get up there," Komorowski replies.

Jerry announces to the group as they enter the aircraft, "I do know Morse code, and I have the fastest fingers east of the Mississippi!" The aircrew then chuckle to themselves and as Lieutenant Foster remarks, "George can teach you how to use the chute, if we have to hit the silk."

At 1140 the men board their planes and proceed through their instrument checks. More tired radial engines of the B-25's cough to life. The Mitchells begin rolling toward the end of the runway. Inside the cockpit of the lead ship, gleaming in unpainted bear metal, Colonel Kendall prepares for takeoff and gets on the radio. "DUGOUT, this is LEAD, request permission for departure." The reply over his headset was not what he expected. "LEAD, you are to hold…We have a delay…"

Kendall starts his inquiry, "Why?"

The radio operator answers "A B-25 at our sister group piled it in at the end of the runway. No one was killed, but they have to move the wreck out of the way with a dozer. Hold position." The colonel tries to hide his disappointment and replies to ground control "Copy LEAD!" The colonel then briefs the rest of his aircraft as to the delay and gets off the radio. He then turns to his copilot to express his disgust.

"You know, first they tell us that we have to rush in to take out a target and now this!" Kendall angrily remarks to his copilot. "Now we have to fly like were at the Cleveland Air Races to make up for the lost time. Lieutenant, show me the flight plan. Maybe we can cut a few corners." His copilot stares at him and quietly remarks, "Maybe the weather boys were right, we should think about postponing, canceling this sucker until the weather clears." Kendall stares out the aircraft window for a period of reflection. His right-seater continues, "It is certainly not a good omen, Sir." Irritation builds in the squadron commander as he squirms a bit in his seat harness.

He fires a broadside in reply. "Well... screw the weather! I know I'm right! I fly by my guts and always have! The Japs will be there as advertised, and I will personally sink all of those bastards! Not a word more about it Lieutenant." The copilot then quietly nods in agreement.

The news of the flight delay is too much for George Komorowski to handle. He unbuckles his seat belt, gets off his chair in the rear of *Bugs Bunny*, and promptly paces the floor in distress. "C'mon, another delay, jeepers!" The other crewman with him is confused. "I can't take much more of this waiting." He exchanges glances out both waist gun windows and declares, "Better yet, maybe the mission has been scrubbed. God I hope so." He cues up his mic to speak to the pilot. "Captain, what's going on? Why are we just sitting here? Let's go! Are we aborting takeoff?" Chuck Wozniak watches his comrade in silence. The nerves of the flight crew are at about wits end. Layton responds, "Nope, we're on hold until Kendall gives us the green light. We heard something about a delay in the third group. Just sit back and relax, we will be up shortly." George sits back down in frustration and nervously wiggles his knees together.

In the cockpit of *Bugs*, Layton now, with rarity, vents his own misgivings about the impending raid. "Damn it! We need to get out of here and beat that typhoon. It will be about three hours before we get to those floating tin cans! I bet we get some really stiff headwinds on the way over." His copilot agrees, "Captain, I hope not. We are putting full faith in our weatherman. He should be here to eat his words. Better yet, if we go down, nothing like having the news and weather together in the same life raft. What a story that would be!"

The pilot also adjusts his rear end in the uncomfortable seat and replies, "Sure thing! I'd have that Sergeant Wilson sit right behind us on this mission! If he made a mistake, then that guy dies right along with us!"

On the flight line, Sergeant Johnson and the mechanics watch the group of aircraft standing idle before them. A corporal asked, "What's going on? Why aren't they up yet?"

Johnson replies to the young lad. "I don't know, maybe the storm is too close, maybe someone wet their diapers."

"Who knows...All I know is that if those boys stay out there much longer, those cylinder head temperatures are going to red line and then we will have our work cut out for us tonight pulling engines." He stares at his wristwatch again.

After several more minutes of tension, a crackle over the headset notifies Kendall that the group is cleared for takeoff. He acknowledges the message as a flare from the operations tent flies skyward. The colonel cues up his throat microphone, "FLIGHT, listen up, we are clear for takeoff, let's go. Let's get these warm eggs to market."

The radio from ground control again reconfirms, "LEAD this is DUG-OUT, you are clear for takeoff and set for a heading of 120 degrees. Good luck and God speed! See you back this evening."

The aircraft take off, one by one, into the cloudless skies of the Solomon Sea. They assemble themselves into formation and begin their long flight of several hours across the ocean. Layton's soiled crew chief Sergeant Johnson jumps on his bicycle and pedals furiously towards the end of the runway as the ground crewmen watch the impressive aircraft formation pass directly overhead. He stops his bike, gets off, and waves at the pilot's crew with his hat. He sees Captain Layton and crew and yells out with excitement, "Go get 'em *Bugs*! Go get 'em man!"

Flight leader Colonel Kendall directs his silver bomber on course toward the target area. The engines drone as the navigators check the flight path as the men man their stations. The airmen scan the skies and ocean for any sign of enemy activity. Nothing is sighted. They breathe a collective sigh of relief. The clouds of the typhoon begin to gather on the horizon. In Layton's B-25 it is just another routine mission.

"I guess the Japs don't think were going to hit them in this weather. Maybe they think we're stupid for trying," remarks top turret gunner Daryl Ford over the interphone. The flight to the convoy proceeds without major trouble, however, a danger from a new quarter manifests itself within the waist of Layton's B-25. Top turret gunner Sergeant Ford folds some paper into elaborate origami paper figures of extravagant birds to pass the time. Argendizo watches with interest.

George Komorowski, veteran of numerous missions with the 823rd, once again fights off waves of nervousness and sweat within the cramped confines of his waist gun position. He shifts his weight between both 50-caliber machine guns in the bomber's waist position and loosens his flak vest. Claustrophobia festers itself on the poor airman. He begins to mutter to himself, "Today is our day... I can feel it." The airman glances out both windows again and curses, "Why me! Why me, Lord!" In a semi-delusional state he grabs one machine gun, cocks the weapon, and fires a short burst. "Not if I can help it... C'mon you bastards, I'm waiting, come to Uncle George. I'll give you one right across the ass!" The weapon discharges again and is heard throughout the aircraft. Ed Layton gets on the interphone and yells "Who's firing?!" More bursts are heard. Sergeant Wozniak radios back to the pilot, "Captain we got a problem. George is losing it back here, someone's going to get hurt!"

Ed Layton yells out, "George, what's going on? Answer me! Stop firing!" The gunfire ends. Komorowski answers, "I can't take it anymore. I've got to sit down. Today we're going to get it. I can feel it... Please...turn around before we all get..." Layton interrupts abruptly, "Can't do that George!" The captain hears silence over the headset. Ed cues the mic again. "Sergeant Wozniak, check on Komorowski. Knock some sense into him." Chuck acknowledges and leaves the tail gun.

The Chicago native is leaning up against the bulkhead in tears. Sergeant Wozniak pats his hand on his comrade's shoulder, trying to get him to regain his senses. "George, what's up? C'mon buddy. Just settle down. We are going to be okay, stop making a silly Axis of yourself...We will be over the target area soon." Komorowski shudders with fright after hearing the word "target." The waist gunner then springs to his feet, looks Chuck in the eye with hysteria, and mutters, "This flight has to be stopped, Chuck. It's got to be stopped. I tell you... We're all going to die! You heard 'Tokyo Rose,' they all got a price on our heads!" ('Tokyo Rose' is a nickname for Axis collaborator and Japanese-American born Iva Toguri D'Aquino, who hosted a radio propaganda program *The Zero Hour* aimed at U.S. troops during the war. Pardoned by President Gerald Ford in 1977. She died in Chicago. Illinois in 2006.)

The crewman begins to cry and mutters, "What about the headhunters on these remote islands! I don't want my shrunken head on the end of a stick! Nooo!" The man is overwhelmed in tears.

Trembling with fright and weeping, the waist gunner stands up, grabs the sergeant and slams him into the bulkhead. Wozniak tries to push his paranoid comrade away, without success. George yells, "I don't want my head at the end of the stick!" He punches Chuck in the stomach, who immediately falls to the plane's floor. The radio silence is too much for the pilot. He orders his top turret gunner to go aft and see what is going on as he begins to retrim the plane's flight controls. The Indian views the commotion and mutters, "What now?" He enters the cabin as Komorowski declares his intentions to stop the flight. Wozniak frantically yells out, "Daryl, get him off of me, damn it!" Ford grabs George in a headlock from behind and drags him off Wozniak. Komorowski breaks free and pushes Sergeant Ford into the back wall and levels a right hook at him, as Ford too falls to the floor.

Moments later, Ford and Wozniak have George cornered, as Sergeant Ford promptly tackles him. The men twist and turn, and Ford calls out for help as Komorowski claws at his face as though demon-possessed. Chuck renders assistance as George refuses to budge with Daryl pinned to the floor. In the cockpit, the silence is too much for the flight crew. Randy cues up the mic, "What in the hell is going on back there? Damn it, get the situation under control...Pronto!"

Wozniak yells out "All right, that's it!" He grabs and turns Komorowski toward him and punches George in the head. The waist gunner rolls over on the floor, dazed and confused. Chuck declares, "You should be court-martialed, thrown out the bomb bay, for the stunt you just pulled! Like it or not, we are all tied up in this together. We're supposed to be a team. Remember!" He helps Sergeant Ford off the floor. Komorowski finally regains his senses, tearfully apologizes, and eventually returns to his post. Daryl Ford reports the situation to the pilot as the crew again focuses on the mission. Wozniak provides the last words of solid encouragement to his troubled comrade. "George. I have flown two missions with you guys so far and with many other planes. From what I see you have a great crew, and we're going to be all right." He bends down slightly and rests his hand briefly on the gunner's shoulder. "You have to trust your combat experience. Besides, if anyone tries to come for your head..." He reaches for his holster, pulls out his Colt-45 pistol, and cocks the gun in front of Sergeant Komorowski, "They are going to have to come through me first. Now get back on your feet, I can't man two gun positions at the same time!"

Argendizo passes the time up until the bomb run by trying to fold elaborate paper airplanes behind the cockpit bulkhead. Daryl then gives the New Yorker some of his pointers.

The Weather Bureau

The weather operations room clock back at the squadron now shows 2:35 P.M. The room is full of action, as to be expected with the tracking of the dangerous inbound weather system. Corporal Berger approaches his boss once again with another radio intercept. "Sergeant Wilson Sir, we just got this weather report from one of the lead B-25's in the second attack group and a coast watcher off Rabaul. It has an air pressure reading that will get your attention." He hands over the notepad, and it is studied intently. Wilson replies, "Corporal, get me the latest copy of the flight plan." The soldier goes over to a map desk, pulls out a copy, and lays it out on the large map table.

A small group gathers around the map table. Sergeant Wilson addresses the group of onlookers. "Crap! The typhoon is moving faster than we thought. We have to alert our group and have them abort the mission. Get them outta there! The air pressure right near the 'Tokyo Express' is below 980 millibars. I have to talk to Lieutenant Colonel Stallings, the wing commander, right now!" He heads out of the tent. One staff member turns to Corporal Berger and remarks, "I don't think anyone is going to listen to him. War is hell."

The Final Approach

The island of New Britain appears on the horizon as the black specks of enemy surface ships en route to Bougainville dot the deep blue sea. The small formation of B-25's of the fourth group make their approach as Commander Kendall and his copilot stare at the ominous clouds before them and then at each other. The brilliant lightning is clearly visible as rain is beginning to collect on the windscreen. Kendall glances at his watch. The veteran commander spots the convoy of enemy ships below and the departing planes of the third group. The colonel's radio headset erupts to life "THIRD BASE to HOME-PLATE, we are leaving the INFIELD. Good luck. Over! Repeat, this is THIRD BASE to..." (static from lightning blocks transmission) ...leaving the INFIELD..." Winds reported at thirty-five to forty knots out of the northwest with rain squalls on the INFIELD, Batter up!" A big lightning bolt strikes nearby, drowning out the rest of the message, "Batt... Up!" meaning the fourth group is clear to attack the convoy.

Colonel Kendall cues up his mic and promptly answers, "THIRD BASE this is HOME PLATE, we are entering the INFIELD. HOME PLATE entering the INFIELD over!" The commander looks at his copilot, also wrestling with the flight controls, and says, "Son of a gun! Winds near 40 knots! It will slow us down over those ships. I hope we're not going to be sitting ducks. John, check our fuel. We might have to open up the throttles a bit. Nothing like having the raid driven by the weather forecast huh?" with a slight chuckle. The copilot is not amused in the least, wishing the raid was aborted. "Here we go." Layton cues up the radio to radio his formation, "Men, all right we are going in. Get into attack formation. Here we go!"

The B-25's line up in attack formation. Inside the cockpit of *Bugs Bunny,* the pilots listen to their strike leader's garbled transmission. "Men, we're going in. Get ready and watch for enemy fighters…heavy flak!" Colonel Kendall cues up his mic and then yells out over interphone, "All right guys, look sharp! Man your stations, watch for enemy fighters! It is starting to look really nasty outside and this could be more bumpy than normal. Fire short bursts to conserve ammunition. Watch for enemy fighters!"

Jerry watches as Daryl Ford quickly takes his origami and stuffs them into his leather flight bag and mounts his seat to man the bomber top turret gun. Layton is very concerned about the weather as he looks at the dark cloud formations that lay ahead and comments, "Look at those clouds. All hell is about to break loose. See the lightning?" Smoke clouds of damaged ships darken the maddening sky. Layton then turns to his trusty copilot and yells out, "All right Randy! Let's give her the gas and see what this aircraft is made of! Let's follow Kendall in; he is off to the right in the silver bullet!"

Lieutenant Foster is excited, with adrenaline pumping through his veins, and answers appropriately, "Roger that Captain, we're going in!" Angry bursts of flak from Japanese destroyers greet the last wave. Foster comments, "I wish we could go back to hitting ground targets. Christ! There's nothing to hide behind. They can define their lead on us before we even get over them!" The aircraft scores several hits as an ammunition ship erupts into a bright ball of flame. Two B-25's plunge into the sea ablaze on the 823rd's first run. Layton reminds his copilot, "Keep your eyes peeled for those destroyers, Randy, find us a juicy target! The rain is getting heavy. See anything?" The bomber's tail and waist gunners open fire on the enemy ships, hitting valuable cargos lashed to their decks.

The Mitchell bombers continue to drop their 500-pound bombs. After releasing their loads, the aircraft return to strafe their prey with their nose mounted 50-caliber machine guns. The angry storm clouds of the typhoon make their presence known as lightning streaks over the convoy. Rain blankets the ships as Layton glides *Bugs Bunny* towards a large tanker. All eyes are on the target vessel. Another B-25, *Ace of Spades*, follows behind *Bugs* as Foster then tells his pilot, "Hit this baby, and the well will run dry at every Jap airfield in the area. That's for sure!" The pilot opens fire with the nose-mounted guns of the B-25's. Tex's hand firmly grips the bomb release lever as the tracer bullets rake the bridge of the luckless tanker. Lieutenant Foster then yells out "Bombs away!" as the bombs hurl downward towards the target.

Both Mitchells laid a string of bombs on the target. Within seconds the tanker is ablaze and explodes in spectacular fashion. The pilots in their aircraft look at each other with jubilation as their target is annihilated. Lieutenant Foster comments as he opens the logbook and readies his pencil, "Let me enter this into our logbook. Let's see, position 6 degrees south, 154 degrees east. "Sighted ship sank same!" Oh brother, how have you ever made it out of grammar school?" Captain Layton laughs aloud.

News reporter Argendizo is staring forward watching the pilots on the next attack run and scribbles notes in his pocketbook commenting "Sighted ship sank same, I like that." He suddenly looks up and backs away from the cockpit as it is illuminated by a bright burst of lightning, shouting, "Yeow! You guys normally fly through this stuff?" as he tries to clear his eyes of spots. The bomber rocks violently with the crack of thunder. Copilot Foster answers in comical fashion with his eyes closed from the burst of light, "Jerry, what do you mean? This is good weather! There won't be any enemy fighters out there to turn us into Swiss cheese!" Argendizo then shouts, "Holy Mary, full of grace!" and then makes the sign of the cross.

A minute later the keen-eyed Texan, spots a freighter off to the left slowly being enveloped in a rainsquall, and he comments, "Ed, a freighter making a run for it to the east, ten o'clock about a mile away!" Layton stares at his fuel gauge.

Foster keeps up the pressure. "C'mon, let's go get 'em! He isn't zig-zagging. Probably thinks we can't see 'em. We got plenty of 50's to light him up!" Lightning exposes the ship beneath a wall of rain. "Yeah, I see him; I will bring us down to about 200 feet, so we can put the pepper on him with the guns. Randy, if I can just hold this bucket of bolts steady! Give me a hand!" Layton remarks.

Layton noses the B-25 to the east and begins his attack run. Red tracer bullets wisk by the aircraft as it dives on the ship. Several bullets strike the cockpit and instrument panel of the bomber as *Bugs* lets loose with a roar of her own guns. Ed's aim proves perfect as multiple strikes are seen on the fore-castle of the helpless merchant ship. Fires break out among the trucks and jeeps lashed to her deck. The bomber veers off at roughly 50 feet above the waves in the angry wind and rain. The lucky rabbit's foot had indeed saved the daring aircraft, at least for now. The Associated Press reporter has one hell of a story so far!

The crew of Layton's aircraft celebrate their latest victory but fail to rec-ognize an oncoming deadly Japanese *Fubuki Class* destroyer. Tex Foster's keen eyes again seem to prevail as he shouts alarm. "Ed watch it! Destroyer on the left! Turn hard right! Oh Lord, he's got us now!" The B-25 begins a perilous climb as both pilots duck and cover their heads. The bomber is hit with cannon fire all along her entire length and suddenly pitches downward. The altimeter indicator on the instrument panel dives. George in the waist gun position leaps for cover as bullets rip just below his feet. The pilots grab the control column as the aircraft almost hits the waves below them. They successfully recover from the unexpected dive. The weather is ferocious as high winds grip the plane.

The pilots examine themselves for injuries and find Layton's arm cut by shrapnel and Lieutenant Foster some scratches. Jerry Argendizo heads aft to check on the rest of the crew. Randy presses the pilot to relinquish control of the aircraft, but the request is denied. An irritated Lieutenant Foster then heads back to get the first aid kit for his injured pilot. The top turret gunner gets a few words in along the way. "Lieutenant Sir, everything okay up front? I heard a few bullets strike home. Hey, you're bleeding!" The sergeant points it out to the copilot.

Tex is smoldering with anger and replies, "I'll be okay, I got cut up a bit, *but* that pilot of ours is sure something! His arm is sliced open, and he *still* insists on flying this bird, rather than let me have a crack at it!"

A small smile appears on the Indian's face as he utters, 'Well, I guess rank has its privileges!" Lieutenant Foster has had enough of it and blurts out, "Shut up." Sergeant Ford suddenly realizes the slip in words and feels absolutely miserable. The newsman enters the rear cabin with a first aid kit and tends to the wounded. Chuck Wozniak has moderate shrapnel wounds that require immediate attention, after his position took a pasting. George assists Jerry in applying a dressing to stem Chuck's bleeding, while the gunner sits behind his rearward facing 50-caliber machine guns.

The Flight into Oblivion

The aircraft is damaged; however, *Bugs* manages to stay airborne in the clawing wind and rain. The Mitchell strafes one last target and begins to be enveloped by the typhoon. A thick sheet of rain covers the area, with visibility at an absolute minimum. Randy finishes bandaging up his pilot's injury. Ed Layton presents his damage assessment over the interphone, "Lieutenant, the leading edge of the right wing is damaged with holes. Both engines look good from here, still running. So far we don't need to reach for the rabbit's foot. See any other bombers?" The tail gunner quickly reports in. "No Sir! The rain is too thick!" Layton then prepares an impromptu roll call. "All right men, a check of battle stations, report in. Top turret? "Sir top turret good!" Daryl belts out with enthusiasm.

"Waist gun, how are you looking back there George? See any of our group buddy?" Komorowski steps to the clear glass window and is a bit unnerved when he spots damage to the aircraft.

"No sign of the rest of our tigers, but ah, the right side has some good holes near the window, the floor is full of holes. Both engines seem good from back here. If they are leaking, I can't tell in the heavy rain." Both the pilot and copilot try to keep cool as the inventory of crew continues. The newsman sits in the entry to the cockpit and breathes a sign of relief with each report. Layton continues, "Wozniak. How are things looking in the tail? Do we still have one?"

The crewman in the rear compartment answers with apprehension. "Sir, we have damage to the control surfaces. Half the rudder is missing on the right side. The left side of the tail is good. My wounds have been taken care of Sir."

The pilot then remarks, "No wonder it feels like we are a bustling bronco up here." The damage assessment continues from Wozniak, "The elevator is pretty chewed up and a slug went right through my left hand. It hurts like hell and the bleeding is now under control. I'll live. It is getting really bumpy back here, and I am getting out of my position. No enemy fighter spotted!"

The wounded gunner carefully slides himself out of the cramped tail gun position. George assist Chuck from the rear tail position, and check the gunner for any additional wounds.

"Job well done Sergeant. You and George can stand down. There is no further sight of the enemy. Maybe the typhoon sank what's left."

In the bomber cockpit, the airmen now set about the task of trying to identify the safest path back to the formation of bombers. The copilot has just returned to his seat. "Randy, I have no idea where we are. See if you can get us some kind of bearings. The formation has made a run for it. We've been left behind. It looks like our directional instruments took a real pasting. I think our clock is all that is working now. We do have a great tailwind, to slingshot us out of here, to who knows where." "Jerry!"

The newsman quickly springs to life. "Yes Captain!"

"While you are back there, give me a status on the condition of the life raft and flares. We may have to ditch." Ed Layton remarks, with an ominous tone.

"You can count on me Sir, be back in a flash." The reporter then exits the cockpit. Lieutenant Foster pulls out his map in the cockpit. "Without any means of a compass, I guess we just have to pull over on the side of the road and just ah... ask. "'Cap, our current position is at, I believe 6 degrees South, 154 degrees east, on a heading of 315 degrees north. I suggest you make that turn to get us back to the Southeast, at 225 degrees...'" The pilot stares out his window into the heart of the storm and replies, "Good course of action." He fights the angry wind holding firmly on the control column. "I will start to make that turn, damn this blasted wind!"

Captain Ed Layton has always been known for keeping his aircrews fully up to date on the current flight status of his aircraft. Today is certainly no exception. He cues up his microphone and delivers his news update. "Guys, have your Mae Wests ready. (U.S. military issue life preserver, named after shapely Hollywood actress Mae West). I don't know how much longer we will be in the air. I am noticing a drop in oil pressure in engine number two, and the cylinder head temperatures are rising. Also, we are dropping fuel on the right side. I will try to use as much gas as we can before I hit the wing fuel shut off valve. The shrapnel must have really gotten us on that side. I will try and radio the formation." Sergeant Ford leaves his top turret position and enters the door to the cockpit. He is horrified by the damage to the cockpit instrumentation.

The captain now makes an attempt to contact the rest of the aircraft by radio. It is doubtful that any conversation will be likely in the harrowing storm. "This is *Bugs Bunny* 265217 to LEAD, acknowledge. Have lost all compass and navigation equipment and flying blind. We need the formation. Anybody! Over." There is no reply, except for the sound of lightning spikes and static on the radio loudspeaker. "Repeat! Aircraft 265217, have lost all navigation equipment, we need the formation. Over!" Captain Layton gives up and glances at his trusty copilot. The top turret gunner remarks, "Now we know what it means to fly by the seat of our pants." The pilot tries not to show any signs of panic and says, "You got that right Sergeant. We are holding our own for the moment. I don't know for how much longer. This tail wind is now just pushing us off in some direction."

Suddenly the B-25 begins to shudder violently. Layton stares at the instrument panel and sees the oil pressure on the number two engine drop to zero. He announces his immediate action, "We have lost oil in engine two… got to feather it right now!" The pilot grabs the feather lever on the control column and actuates it. The propeller blades on the engine then turn into a position to prevent turbulence from the winds from causing the plane to crash. "I have to re-trim this cripple again."

In the departing bomber formation, group leader Kendall mentally tallies the remaining planes around him as the storm trails the group. The colonel asks the formation if they can find the other missing B-25's. The radio springs to life with sad news. "Colonel! We saw two B-25's hit the drink. Cunnigham's *Pacific Raider* exploded, and *Straight Eights* is no longer with us. No parachutes or rafts…no nothing. The *Bugs Bunny* is missing. This is Captain Brock. Over." There is silence in the cockpit of the lead bomber. Colonel Kendall tries to put together the words to console the rest of the bomb group.

"Roger that Captain Brock. Keep a sharp lookout for that straggler. All other aircraft present and accounted for. Maintain our present heading. In a few minutes we will be turning towards New Guinea." Kendall's copilot remarks, "*Bugs*! Why that's Layton's ship. I hope that they can make it back, there aren't any gas stations out here to pull into."

Colonel Kendall has high praise for the lost aircrew and has confidence that the lost B-25 will return home safely. He turns to his comrade, "Yes I know, but Layton has been up this road before. I don't know if you hear the whole story Frank, but the captain was flying a B-26 off the coast of Midway last year. They thought he was a goner, but he always had a knack of surviving. He will find his way home. Layton is one of the best pilots in our group." He cues up the radio to communicate with the rest of the bombers. "All right guys, we're beginning our left turn, on a heading of 270 degrees, follow me…"

For the next hour, the situation in *Bugs Bunny* becomes tense. The strong winds have not only blown the bomber off course but are dangerously affecting the remaining fuel supply. Jerry returns to the cockpit from the rear of the bomber and makes his report. "Captain, the life raft isn't as sturdy as a lifeboat off the Titanic, but it looks good. Not a scratch. George and Wozniak are managing quite well back there, Sir."

The news is good for the crew, as Layton remarks, "That's great, and I think we are going to have to auger it in. It is a blessed miracle that we have stayed up as long as we have and were fortunately not shot down."

The newsman quickly replies, "Well I guess we can thank our lucky rabbit's foot and 'Ole *Bugs Bunny*!" He pats the fuselage skin with enthusiasm. The pilot and copilot stare out into the blackness of night in the storm with growing apprehension.

In the rear of the Mitchell bomber, both crewman settle back in their seats, contemplating their future. George tries to keep from being overcome with fear once again. He turns to his comrade. "Chuck, I am just terrified of sharks. I don't have the guts Jonah had. I might not make it into the boiling kettle of water at the headhunter's party this evening." The tail gunner tries to steer him into the clear. "Now you block that out of your mind! Man, I would give you a cigarette now to calm your nerves, but we don't know if we are leaking fuel. I'd use my lighter and we'd all turn into confetti. I will get you a pack of cigarettes when we land."

In the cockpit, the fuel situation is becoming desperate. *Bugs Bunny* is now flying literally on a wing and a prayer. There is no telling how much fuel will flow through the carburetor on the remaining engine. "Randy, check the right fuel tank. What is it reading?" Layton asked. "Fumes! It contains probably a few pounds of fuel. I don't have my gas ration book with me either!" the Texan remarks, with a slight grin. The captain makes the fateful decision, "Okay, that's what I thought. Close the right wing fuel shut off valve." The copilot then assesses the remaining fuel load. "Captain, judging by the fuel left in the other tanks, I'd say we have about half an hour of flight left. Now, if we toss junk overboard, maybe we can squeeze another gallon or two of liquid courage."

Captain Layton agrees with the fateful decision to lighten the load as they fly off into oblivion. He gets on the aircraft interphone. "Men, listen up. As you know, we are flying blind, lost in this damn typhoon. We suffered hits on the right side of the plane, and I had to feather engine two. We are low on fuel, and now is the time we start tossing everything out! Quickly gentleman! Keep your Colt-45's. George, Sergeant Wozniak, lose the 50-caliber machine guns and all the ammunition boxes. Toss all that junk out the bomb bay! Right now! Move the raft, radio, and antennae forward away from the tail. Dump the two sets of flares. No one is going to see them in this storm! Daryl and Jerry, find everything that is not bolted down and toss it out. We have to lighten up this bird." Argendizo unhooks a fire extinguisher and then heads for the bomb bay doors.

The pilot turns to his copilot and deduces a new course of action. "Lieutenant, this might be able to buy us some time. Look at the high cylinder head temperatures on number one. The strain is just too much for it." He is gripped with agony and continues. "We have got to find an island, an atoll, a sand bar…something! We have got to get rid of more dead weight."

Sergeant Ford then sticks his head into the cockpit. "Lieutenant Foster, pop open the bomb bay doors!" The officer answers with pleasure and actuates the bomb doors to the fully open position. In the rear empennage of *Bugs Bunny*, the two crewman start to manhandle the ammunition boxes toward the bomb bay. George tells his comrade, "After the stupid thing I did, maybe I should jump out the bomb bay to save us some weight." I heard last night that 'Tokyo Rose' has got a price of 10,000 bucks on each of us." The Chicago native shudders with fright. Wozniak settles down his troubled comrade yet again, "Look George, calm down. We got two good guys in the cockpit, and we'll be okay. Trust me, we're going to make it. Now let's (ugh!) get this ammo overboard." They toss the large crate out the bomb bay, and the ammunition box is devoured by the vicious storm.

The cockpit window is battered in the heavy rain. After several minutes, Captain Layton orders his men into crash positions. The thunder and lightning shake the aircraft as the sight of the waves grows frighteningly clearer into view. The aircraft is losing altitude. The copilot almost has his nose to the side window glass, trying in vain to spot solid earth. Out of the dark gray sky comes the sight of an island, shrouded in a rain squall. Lightning confirms the island's existence.

Lieutenant Foster quickly alerts the crew. "Captain, Captain! I spotted an island! Terra Firma! See it off to the right? At two o'clock low! Oh my God!" His pilot leans over as Tex points with his hand. "There it is Ed! See it? Hallelujah! It looks like a large Atoll, crescent-shaped!" The pilot desperately searches for a place to set his bird down. Engine number one, begins to cough and sputter as it runs on vapors. Layton tells Foster to get ready to feather the prop on one and shut the engine down. With little time to spare, a long stretch of what appears to be shallow beach is framed in the cockpit window. Layton directs the aircraft and makes his final approach, keeping her at a nose high attitude. The crew brace themselves as Layton and Foster tighten their seat harnesses. They struggle with the control yokes in the heavy winds, trying in vain to hold their bird level. Every effort is taken to ensure the *Bugs* will not cartwheel on landing.

In the rear of the B-25, the two crewmen are ecstatic about the discovery of the island. Sergeant Wozniak grabs Komorowski in a headlock and says, "What did I tell you comrade? We are gonna get through this! Thank you Jesus!" George makes the sign of the cross and wipes the tears from his eyes, which are filled with great relief.

Crash Landing.

The captain yells to his crew over the interphone, "We're going in, brace yourselves!" The crew hangs on for dear life.

Lieutenant Foster leads the way. "Ed, it looks like a good place to set her down. The shallows are quite large, water looks like it's less than five-feet deep." The cylinder temperature gauge on the number one engine is indicating in the red arc, meaning an overheat condition. Ed Layton notices that the aircraft engine is going to die with misfiring in the cylinders. Layton touches the engine gauge on the instrument panel before him, in great appreciation for the Wright Aircraft Engine Corporation's durable product. "Thanks for keeping us up this long, I can't ask you for a minute more. Foster, shut down and feather engine one." Argendizo stares at the lucky rabbit's foot hanging in the cockpit and smiles.

Layton spots the beach, pounded by waves, and readies for the final turn as lightning again illuminates the treacherous surf. Layton again makes the final call over the intercom. "Men, brace yourselves for landing! I am going to make a pass over the island and make a graceful left turn. We are coming down in the shallows. There is plenty of beach down there." The captain then sets the plane down tail first in the water and the strong winds. The plane resists the controls and bounces back into the air. "It looks like *Bugs* doesn't want to go for a swim," Foster remarks. Layton eventually gets the tail down as a tremendous jolt is felt inside the plane. The pilot and co-pilot lurch forward, almost eating the instrument panel in the process.

The B-25 hits the water flat on her belly and immediately sheds her tail section. The shearing of the metal fuselage is heard quite audibly. The bomber is eventually halted in the large swells as the crew struggles to gain their wits and try to escape. Water rushes in from the waist gun position windows. The pilot and co-pilot unbuckle their harnesses and pop the escape hatch. Foster's lip is bleeding from the impact. Water fills the fuselage as the remaining men squirm free of the wreckage. Some of the crew is horrified as they watch Sergeant Wozniak being swept away and swallowed up by the waves. He vanishes without a trace. The rest of the crew manages to wiggle free of the sinking bomber and cling to the single life raft.

The raft bounces in the heavy waves as it heads for shore. The pounding surf of the storm torments the survivors. They trudge across the wet beach sand, hide the raft, and walk into the jungle. The drenching downpour, howling wind, and lightning accompany the men on their journey to seek shelter. A flash of lightning reveals the presence of an abandoned missionary school. The men enter and close the door behind them. Layton tells his fellow crewmen, "Not quite the Ritz Carlton Hotel, but it will have to do." Lieutenant Foster closes the window shutters with the help of fellow crewmen. Argendizo finds an old oil lantern and lights it with his cigarette lighter. Sergeant Daryl Ford instinctively takes out his Colt-45 pistol and begins to pull it apart to clean it. Captain Layton surveys the room and sits down in a corner, pondering what tomorrow will bring. He stares at his watch.

"Captain, where do you think we landed?" Komorowski, asks inquisitively. He looks to the copilot. "Lieutenant, any ideas? Hope this is Australia." Foster enters the conversation. "The last time I looked on my map we were near of Rabaul, and that typhoon gave us quite a spin, like being in a washing machine. I bet this island is just crawling with Japanese soldiers. We will be ready for them in the morning…" He continues to clean his weapon. "Head hunters too…"

Captain Layton adds, "Let's all get some good rest. Tomorrow morning we will figure out where we landed. Then we will scrounge around to find us something to eat and drink." The storm begins to subside, as the men succumb to exhaustion and soon fall asleep.

The Mysterious Island

The sun is shining and all is quiet the next morning. The typhoon had finally passed. Captain Layton is the first one to wake up after enduring a frightening dream of having his beloved aircraft blown out from under him off Midway Island. He sits up on the floor and quietly observes his men sleeping before him. Ed stands up and quietly steps outside the building to survey the area. He walks down the stairs, closing the door behind him. The pilot walks a few paces, stepping over palm fronds strewn across the ground.

Several other crewmen wake up and soon leave the old building as well. They join the pilot and reflect on the crazy night before. Captain Layton quietly greets the rest of his crew. "Are you all slept out? I know it was a bit hard last night. It is a miracle that we survived the crash. Let's get going and try to figure this place out. Keep quiet, communicate with hand signals only. For all we know, this place could be another one of *Tojo's* islands. Locked and loaded gentleman? Let's go," the captain remarked.

Readying their side arms, the crew begins to walk and explore the island. The men are just amazed at the island and all its beauty. They examine flowers and sample some of the exotic berries. The men even take some time to refresh themselves with a drink at a picturesque waterfall. They walk for about a mile and then Cherokee Indian Sergeant Daryl Ford makes a unique discovery in the nearby bushes. He calls the crew over with the whistle of a bird. The crew suddenly rush over to him. They stare at the ground with disbelief. He has found an African Lion that had been killed by a falling tree trunk during the storm.

"Ah guys, this doesn't belong here, take a look. I don't know what to say." Daryl says with total confusion.

"Well, maybe this cat swam ashore after a ship sank after breaking out of the cargo hold. Heck, we got here, and so did this animal," George added to the discussion.

Tex merely shakes his head and remarks, "Yeah right, I really doubt it Sergeant. These animals are not known for swimming like Tarzan's Johnny Weissmuller!" The pilot kneels down before the animal and feels the soft fur and comments, "How in the world did this thing get all the way from Africa over here? Unbelievable. Now we know that that there is some kind of intelligent form of life on this island. Let's get going. I wonder what other surprises are lurking out there. If any other creature attacks, by all means blow it away."

Komorowski comically adds, "Maybe we can take this lion home with us, stuff it, and put it in the NCO Club!"

The men resume their march through the lush vegetation and deep tropical forest underbrush. They walk to a flowing stream, clean themselves, and drink more water. The journey continues. Jerry Argendizo amuses the group with light quiet conversation. "You know, I could build a nice house here." Komorowski quickly answers with sarcasm, "I wouldn't live here. No Sir. Even if this was Park Place, I wouldn't buy it for $350. One would have to be crazy to build something here. I spent some R & R in Hawaii, on Oahu, and I do get Island Fever."

The New Yorker Argendizo continued, "No really I mean it. It is so quiet and peaceful. I could have a nice hut on the beach, sure beats Brooklyn. This jungle is better than the concrete one. Who knows, there might be some nice women slinking around here." Lieutenant Foster decides to get in a quick swipe at the press agent, "Jerry I give you a million bucks if you find a hula girl in this 'paradise.'" Argendizo, the avid card player, admits defeat. "Lieutenant, for once you are right, you'd probably clean my chips right off the poker table on that one!"

"Guys, I don't know about you, but I am starting to get really hungry. We either have to catch some fish or shoot a bird or lion. C'mon don't tell me you guys aren't hungry!" George laments.

The Texan agrees with the sergeant, "I would like to have a nice thick steak with baked beans and mashed potatoes. Hell, let's go rustle up one of those cattle, that jungle oxen. It's around here in these parts isn't it? Lord knows I saw pictures of them in *National Geographic*, or maybe I was mistaken. I think it might have been in French Indochina. George is right. Let's see if we can hustle up some grub." The Cherokee exclaims, "Yeah, that sounds good, I could build a fire and cook something. My ancestors didn't raise a bunch of dummies you know."

The men continue the seemingly endless trek through the jungle. Suddenly, without warning, George trips off an animal snare and is hoisted airborne and swears in Polish. The men in the group begin to laugh at him as he hangs upside down. Captain Layton tells his men to quiet down. Jerry poses proudly beside George, smiles, and remarks, "You know, I've never seen the stockyards of Chicago until…"

"Oh shut up and get me down!" Komorowski shouts. The men cut the rope and lower George to safety. The aspiring priest mutters more Polish curse words at Argendizo and chases the smiling newsman a short distance after being released.

Layton settles down the situation. "Cool it down guys, save your energy. We may have to make an Olympic dash to freedom from the Japs if we stumble on any of them."

The crew resumes their trek through the jungle, battling insects and cutting more thick underbrush with their knives. They reach a small footpath. Daryl, senses something in the distance and advises caution.

Captain Layton tells his men to spread out and take cover as he cocks his pistol. They throw themselves into the bushes and sit quiet. Voices are heard. The men freeze. A patrol of six Japanese soldiers make their way along the path, talking among themselves. The crew of *Bugs Bunny* holds their fire. The Japanese pass by without incident into the jungle and disappear.

"We're not alone," whispers Foster. Layton nods his head in agreement. He then quietly announces to the group, "Daryl and I will go on ahead. You guys stay down, and we'll be right back. Don't shoot unless fired upon, and for Christ's sake don't shoot us down when we come back!" The sound of an aircraft engine is suddenly heard in the distance.

The two men scurry on ahead and eventually get down on their knees and crawl forward through the dense vegetation. They carefully move the weeds aside and spot several sandbagged aircraft revetments containing three Japanese Zero fighter planes, including another plane carefully camouflaged under a tarp. The men strain to identify the strange fighter but are unsuccessful. It seems that one Zero is undergoing a throttle alignment check with the engine moving through several ranges of performance. Soldiers clear away storm debris from the makeshift runway. Both crewmen then crawl back and notify their colleagues of their findings.

"About two hundred yards ahead is a small airfield. Daryl and I saw some Zeros. Now we know whose real estate we landed on. This isn't Park Place," Layton reports to his men.

George interjects, "What are we going to do now Captain? Surrender so we can get a bite to eat, or blow up the planes and start some fireworks before next year's Fourth of July?"

Lieutenant Foster is irritated by the remark and gives his rebuttal. "Heck no! Sergeant do not even think of such a thing. We can vanish into this jungle and outwit the Japanese any day. I think we should get back to the beach, jump into our raft, paddle our way outta here, and get picked up by one of our submarines."

The crew leaves the area and heads away from the airstrip. Unknown to the group, the dark shadows of enemy soldiers scurry forward to quickly head off the Americans from getting deeper into the unforgiving jungle. An ambush is quietly being set. The enemy is a mere twenty-five feet from the men of *Bugs Bunny* as they pause for another rest break in the stifling heat. Lieutenant Foster is suffering miserably in the humidity. "I think that we are going to have to get us some water. This heat is just killing me." He wipes the drops of sweat from his forehead. "We have to hustle off to that brook to get us some. Pronto."

His pilot agrees, "You're right. In this jungle all of us can also catch malaria or dengue fever. Let's sit here for a moment longer to get our strength back, then head back for that waterfall."

Capture!

Sergeant Ford takes several steps away from the resting group. He stops and surveys the rainforest before him. His eyes point skyward to see the magnificent jungle canopy above him and also follow the exotic waterfowl singing in the immediate vicinity. All of a sudden his sixth sense alerts him to trouble. His nostrils flair slightly as if he has picked up a strange scent. There is something out there. The crewman, not to arouse suspicion, carefully scans his eyes along ground level, seeing if he can spot an undetected elusive enemy. One concealed Japanese soldier gently glides out his shiny knife from his uniform belt. The momentary glint of sunlight off that impressive knife catches the Cherokee's eye. From under the leaves and twigs, the shape of an enemy soldier emerges. Daryl suddenly whistles gently to get his colleagues attention. Lieutenant Foster recognizes the danger signal immediately. "Hey Sergeant Ford, you see anything?" Ford suddenly draws his pistol and blasts away at the source of the light, and a Japanese soldier flinches, screams out in pain, and dies within a second.

Suddenly the jungle springs to life. A group of well-camouflaged Japanese troops leap out and overwhelm the B-25 crewmen. Before Sergeant Ford can fire more shots, he is tackled to the ground by another soldier. The Americans are subdued with rifle butts, knives to the throat, and kicks to the head to end all resistance. The Japanese drag Sergeant Ford in brutal fashion by his combat boots and toss him at the feet of their comrades. Captain Layton and Lieutenant Foster have their weapons confiscated. Sergeant Komorowski suddenly drops down to help Daryl and is promptly clobbered on the head with another rifle butt and is unconscious. The Italian-American from the tough streets of Brooklyn, Argendizo, has resisted in magnificent fashion, but with three enemy soldiers pinning him to the ground, the game is over for the A.P. reporter.

One Japanese soldier prods his rifle barrel menacingly close to Captain Layton's mouth. The soldier taunts him by faking pulling the trigger, smiling, and then making the sound of a gunshot. The crewmen are brought to their feet and force-marched along a footpath. Lieutenant Foster and Jerry carry two unconscious crewmen between them. They sweat profusely in the intense heat and humidity. The column of men is herded aboard a small truck that has pulled alongside the roadway. The men are forced aboard and soon drive off into an unknown destination.

The prisoners are driven along the bumpy road through the jungle. The drive allows Sergeants Ford and Komorowski to regain consciousness. One soldier rips the metal pilot's wings from Lieutenant Foster's uniform, eliciting a mean facial expression from the copilot. The soldier takes the wings as a souvenir and places them into his uniform shirt pocket for safe keeping. The reporter sees the incident and is also enraged at the scene. He then gets an idea. As the truck bounces along the road, Argendizo pick-pockets one soldier of his knife in the cramped truck bed.

The vehicle passes by a small platoon of Japanese troops marching along the road. They glance up and are surprised by their first sight of Americans. In the dense jungle the Americans spot what appears to be a small depot containing rows of 55-gallon fuel drums. Native laborers roll some of the barrels and organize them into rows beneath a camouflaged wooden shelter. They look suspiciously light for being labeled as petroleum products and are handled with relative ease while being stacked. The men spot several rice paddy fields in a clearing being tended by natives and oxen.

The truck enters the confines of a small Japanese garrison. There is a building in the compound with a thatched roof that is being repaired from the storm damage the previous night. The guards get the prisoners off the truck and herd them into a courtyard. They stand in the hot sun with their arms raised and hands on their heads. A figure inside the doorway of the building comes forward out of the shadows. The men watch as a Japanese officer, interrupted while shaving, quietly walks down the porch steps. The aircrew is guarded by at least ten soldiers, some with their guns drawn. Sweat rolls down the foreheads of each crewman as they await their fate. All is quiet. The jungle is all that is heard.

The Japanese officer, Colonel Hideo Yakashi, walks to the prisoners and begins to speak, asking for the commanding officer to step forward. The aircrew stand bewildered. He begins to shout at the Americans as he paces around them. The colonel summons a soldier to his side. "Soldier, where did you find these men? I didn't hear any enemy aircraft."

The corporal responds, "Sir! We caught them a short distance from our airfield. We have no idea how they managed to land on the island. We will search the beaches for any boat they may have used."

The officer then stares directly into the eyes of the dispirited, broken crewman. He again speaks out, shouting "Will the commanding officer please step forward!" There is no reaction, the language barrier is apparently too much to breach.

Colonel Yakashi shouts once again, "I will let you stand out here all day until you airmen tell me who is in charge!"

Randy gathers the courage to speak out to his pilot, "I think he is asking for our head officer to step forward." A soldier menacingly prods a bayoneted rifle towards the copilot with the end of his sentence. Captain Layton then drops his hands from his head and takes a few steps toward the colonel. Two soldiers rush forward on either side of the pilot. Yakashi walks forward to stand face-to-face with the captain. The pilot renders a salute, which is returned by the colonel, and renders a hardly heartfelt greeting to Captain Layton. "Looks like I finally got my answer. You pilots are a pathetic bunch!" The Americans react to the perfect English with a slight flinch. The officer continues, "Chickens you are! Hit us and then fly away. Oh no, now you're going to have to stand and fight." He laughs smugly to himself. "You have no wings to carry you away," shaking his head with great confidence. "No, this time you can't get away. I need your name, rank, and serial number." Layton stands defiantly before him in silence. Colonel Yakashi leans forward to look into the eyes of the pilot and yells. "Talk!"

The officer realizes he is getting nowhere. With the simple nod of his head, stepping off to the side, one soldier comes up from behind, takes his rifle butt to whack out the legs from under the pilot. Layton then collapses in pain. Jerry takes one step forward in anger. A rifle gets pointed towards him by another soldier as a warning. Two soldiers then manhandle the pilot back onto his feet. One grabs Layton by the hair and pulls his head up. The colonel bends over and puts his hands on his knees to stare down the pilot, awaiting his answer. Ed Layton manages just a few words while in terrible pain. "Layton, Edward, Captain, serial 5404737..."

Yakashi is quite pleased and manages a weak smile as he stands up. "Now Captain...Layton... what is your unit?" The tough Wisconsinite refuses to answer anymore questions. The officer summons a staff car as the rest of the prisoners are headed for a bamboo stockade prison, lined with barbed wire and strung up with trip wires and hand grenades. There will be no escape. Captain Layton gets aboard the staff car with the colonel at gunpoint, and they are soon on their way to a discreet location. The remaining crewmen watch as the stockade door is slammed in their faces. What will happen to their pilot? Lord only knows.

The Baron

The vehicle drives down the road, eventually halting before another compound with several adjoining huts. The soldiers grab the captain and move him toward the main building. The colonel accompanies the captain as they walk through the door. He hears a piano playing Frederic Chopin's "Polonaise in A-Flat Major." They walk on the wooden floor as the sounds of women laughing lightens the tense atmosphere. The two men enter the room. The captain is amazed to find a westerner, in the company of an exotic Indian women.

The man is seated at his piano with three pretty women seated beside him. The piano virtuoso finishes playing Chopin's "Polonaise," reaches for his wine glass, and finishes his last sip. The women and a Japanese guard smile and applaud the impromptu concert. When they see the colonel, the smiles vanish and the soldier quickly snaps to attention. The stranger notices the American pilot standing in the entranceway to his elaborate master study and waves him forward. "Well what have we here?" the man asks inquisitively.

"An American pilot, his name is Captain Layton. My troops captured him and his crew near our airfield. The others are locked up in the stockade."

The mere mention of more crewmen whets the appetite of this strange pianist. "There are more? Wonderful." The man steps forward from the piano to greet the pilot. "My name is Baron Carl Vandermeer..." The baron extends his hand for a cordial handshake, and it is, of course, refused. "It is most unfortunate that you landed on our island." The Dutchman paces around the American like he's a lab specimen, noting height, physical build, and condition. "However. I'm sure you will welcome this little escape from the war. How did you get here? I didn't know that you had any aircraft out this far. Must have been a hellacious storm you've flown through. Looks like you need a bit of a rest break. I'd like to give you a little tour of this island before you are returned to your men." Colonel Yakashi remarks, "I would advise against that." The baron seems confident in the situation and continues, "Colonel, I don't think it will cause any harm. These Americans have nowhere to go. They are trapped for now, facing only one alternative." He clears his throat, insinuating a horrible fate. Yakashi knows what he means. The man reaches for his glass once again as an Indian woman graciously refills it for him. The pilot stares at the superb hunting trophies on the walls of the elaborate study.

"You have some nice trophies on the wall, especially the buffalo. It is the largest I have ever seen, probably the most dangerous to hunt. Did you have a cannon to take it down?" Ed Layton speaks for the first time.

The Dutchman laughs briefly and responds, "Oh no my dear fellow, the buffalo is not the most dangerous animal on this island." Now the pilot remembers the strange jungle encounter.

"Oh yes, I forgot. When we first landed here some of my men did come across a dead African lion, crushed under a tree trunk from the storm." The baron is saddened and remarked "Oh is that where my little pussy cat ended up? No wonder I didn't see him this morning. Oh what a pity."

Captain Layton continued, "It is obviously not an indigenous species to this..."

"Oh you know about exotic wildlife, splendid," the baron interrupts.

"What else have you imported Vandermeer? Hippos, rhinos, or tigers?" Colonel Yakashi is offered a cool drink and accepts with pleasure as the discussion continues before him.

The baron now continues the rather interesting conversation. "Hunting tigers ceased to interest me years ago. They are a boring lot. I import some animals for amusement purposes from time to time, yes, but they are no match for a hunter with a high-powered rifle and telescopic sight."

Layton asserts himself, "I used to hunt and track black bears in Northern Wisconsin, prior to…" the pilot looks at the colonel, "the whole Pearl Harbor affair."

The Dutchman's interest in the American grows. "I am bitterly disappointed. God created the heavens and the earth and all its creatures they say. I have prayed to him, and he sent me something that now poses a new challenge. I mastered all his animals' captain. They have no chance against me. All they have are instincts. Instinct is no match for reason."

Ed Layton takes a jab at the man, "I'd like to see you swim with sharks."

In the bamboo stockade, the airmen examine their new surroundings. It contains a single hut, furnished with primitive bunks. The news reporter and copilot pace about the enclosure. Tex is not impressed by the accommodations and remarks, "A real El cheapo version of Sing Sing Prison, eh Jerry?"

The New Yorker responds with optimism, "We got to bust on out of here, I'm thinking…"

"Well think faster," Lieutenant Foster answers with great concern. Komorowski sits on his bunk and by chance spots something under the sand. His hands uncover a soiled uniform hidden under his bed. He shakes off the heavy sand and unfolds a jacket before his fellow crewman and remarks, "Hey, look at this, a Royal Air Force uniform. I wonder what happened to this guy?"

Argendizo answers in a sinister fashion, "The Japanese probably fed him to the local headhunters, maybe even shrunk his head." He then eyes George with a devious smile and announces, "Maybe we're next!"

Foster cautions the newsman, "Oh knock it off, quit scaring the lad, even though it would make great headlines back in New York. I can see it now, Jerry Robinson Crusoe, eaten by the cannibals on a deserted island!"

In the Baron's bungalow, the discussion continues, "Well, what do you hunt now?"

The pilot asks inquisitively. "I have created a new animal," the baron replies.

Layton interrupts, "Oh, you are like Dr. Frankenstein. Did you see the Boris Karloff movie? He robs graves and brings the dead back to life."

The baron smiles then laughs. "Oh no, my dear fellow, I am a man of culture, the arts... not a mad doctor. Please consider yourself my guest. Like I said, let me show you the island. Then you will be returned to your crew. Colonel, let me borrow two of your men for an impromptu safari."

Yakashi signals a mild agreement but briefs the soldiers prior to his departure. "Accompany the prisoner. Keep him in sight at all times. If he escapes, the baron will tell you what to do next. You have been through this before." Salutes are exchanged and the colonel leaves. Layton wonders what it was all about and shakes his head with bewilderment.

The Tour

The discussion ends as the men get into the scout car and leave the compound. They drive roughly a mile, and at the command of Vandermeer in Japanese, the car grinds to a sudden halt. A large lizard clumsily walks across the road before them. Carl remarks, "Ah the *Varanus Komodoensis,* the Komodo Dragon, the world's largest lizard...an awesome predator and scavenger. Mr. Layton, it has specialized teeth and strong jaws capable of crushing your thigh or taking down a water buffalo. We almost ran over the poor fellow."

The pilot now sees his moment to get another jab in. "Poor fellow! Ah, so that's how the heads managed to get on the wall of your study!?" The baron's long-winded monologue has been briefly disrupted.

The car drives on, passing a heavily camouflaged building containing fuel drums. Layton again takes notice of the workmen and the white powder—raw opium—being filled into drums with false bottoms. The baron narrates the informal tour. "I used to be a petroleum engineer with Royal Dutch Shell in the East Indies. I left my work and set out to seek my own fortunes in the islands. The spice trade interested me at one time, but it is now in decline. Several of these islands, such as this one and the one next door, do have phosphate deposits that are quite valuable. I intend to develop them after the war is over. Oh yes, the war, how soon we forget." Now for the grand finale, the pilot braces himself for another lecture of sorts.

"When you leave this island captain, there's one thing I would like for you to remember. War is a business. It always was and still is to this day. In America, Kaiser turns out his Liberty Ships, while in Europe Vickers and Krupp build their tanks and guns. When I see an opportunity, I take full advantage of every situation, like in chess. While this world is tearing itself apart in war, I slither in like a snake and corner a sizeable chunk of the narcotics market in South East Asia. My rogue, phantom fleet as it were, quietly transports my raw opium from Hong Kong and Shanghai to transfer points in the Indies. Next year I will enter the markets of Rangoon and Karachi with competitive pricing."

The captain comments, "I saw those rather light drums being filled with something. A white powder." "Quite observant captain, you do have keen eyesight, another valuable asset. Instead of the complicated oil-cracking process, I have developed a far more efficient method of my own for processing and smuggling my white gold. The fuel drums have false bottoms quite naturally." The baron tries his best to impress the American pilot.

"You unfortunately landed on top of one of my facilities. It is with this money that I buy influence in foreign governments and military circles to protect my investments. No one would ever believe that the son of a humble magistrate from Utrecht, Holland could someday amass such a fortune as I have. I may plan to retire quite comfortably there. Who knows, maybe I'll buy the Dutch government."

The Axis

The car resumes its drive through the thick jungle on the narrow winding road. It stops as a group of men emerge from the bushes. A naval officer and soldiers approach the car. Layton recognizes the camouflage uniforms immediately as those of the dreaded German *Waffen S.S.* and surprisingly, members of the Pro-Axis Free Indian Legion in German-style desert uniforms. They are brandishing the latest German weaponry. *What are the S.S. and these guys doing here?* he wonders to himself. He is very disturbed and confused by the whole meeting. Carl greets the officer/engineer with a cordial handshake "*Ah Guten Tag Herr Admiral Brand* (good day Admiral Brand), how is your work progressing this afternoon?"

"Very well *Herr Vandermeer.*" replies the naval officer. "Have all of your equipment and engineers arrived safely from Germany?" Carl asks inquisitively.

"*Jawohl,* (yes) our project is almost complete and we should be ready to begin preliminary testing. The transmitter will arrive soon by U-boat. The research team from Japan has also arrived. Naval headquarters in Berlin is most anxious about our progress. We mustn't keep the *Fuehrer* waiting. He and Admiral Doenitz are quite anxious about our project. After two years of hard work, we're almost finished." The officer now acknowledges the prisoner, "Who's the airman...an American? *Reichsmarshall* Goering says the American people are only good for building Chevrolets, nothing more.

Layton quickly replies, "Yes, I'm an American, and those Chevrolets you mentioned are just flying over Europe as we speak. They'll find and bomb your Volkswagen plants... it is only a matter of time." The engineer loses his smile. The baron watches the colorful conversation with enjoyment. Captain Layton gets in the last word. "I see that the influence of *Herr Hitler* is beginning to spread to the Punjab as well!" One Indian soldier pulls out a knife, but his commanding officer holds him back.

"I will have some more camouflage netting available for your men *Herr Admiral* to cover the storm damage. There may be more Allied reconnaissance planes in the area soon. We would not want this to disturb your work." The baron continues.

"Danke schoen" (thank you) replies the naval engineer, and after a brief handshake, the men return to a jungle trail. The scout car drives onward. The Indian officer speaks with his men. "Sergeant Patel, let's comb the jungle to see if there are any more stragglers. Remember what happened to the last plane that was shot down over the island."

The sergeant acknowledges, "Yes Major, plenty aboard that one." The men of the Indian legion are soon on their way into the jungle.

Major Bhavnani, the hand-picked officer for this special security detail on the lonely Pacific Island, comments on their deployment. "Men, even though we haven't seen any direct combat action, our reports back to Dehli and Premier Chandra Bose have been met with great enthusiasm. He salutes our deployment. Whatever effort we can make here will help us to rid our homeland of the damned British!"

One soldier comments with enthusiasm, "I am so glad that the Germans got us out of their prison camp in North Africa, rescued from our fellow British prisoners. I can't stand them. They ignored us like we didn't even exist."

Another soldier adds, "My family was in virtual bondage to the English;

my mom and dad labored as servants for the local magistrate. The man was brutal, even hit my mother repeatedly. My father stood there and could do nothing. Helpless" The group of men curse the incident.

"I guess the Germans recognize talent when they see it," Major Bhavnani adds in conclusion.

For the German contingent, previously serving with the crack 2nd SS Panzer Division 'Das Reich', the assignment has been met with extreme boredom. Having been withdrawn from the brutal Russian front, this platoon of veterans battle nothing more now than mosquitoes and vermin on the island. They assist the German navy for a planned secret operation. The Germans, always known for extreme security measures, snagged these combat elite to protect a major investment in the war effort on a truly global scale. Morale could be judged as a level above complete misery. A short-wave radio and maybe letters from home delivered by a Japanese or German submarine passing through the area is their only contact with Nazi Germany.

The Secret Revealed

In Colonel Yakashi's scout car, Captain Layton is beginning to see the whole picture. "So.... I see that you've maintained your contacts with the *Vaterland* (Fatherland). I'm not used to seeing Nazis and some of their new friends this close up, apart from the ones in newsreels, goose stepping across…" Layton remarked. The Dutchman quickly cuts him off, "Yes, I know, I have seen them up close as well, when they marched through my native Holland. Luckily they afford my business operation world class protection. As you can see Captain, I have friends in high places."

"More like the stuff I remove from the bottom of my boots at the end of the day," the airman quietly mutters to himself.

The car drives for a few minutes, then rolls to a halt. Ahead of them in the dense jungle is a clearing. Everyone steps from the car. The rifle of a Japanese soldier prods Captain Layton. German and Japanese civilian engineers are seen assembling near a large circle of antennas that will surround a central transmitter.

"Observe, Mr. Layton, the latest in German ingenuity in the field of electronics. The men call it *Merkur*, Mercury, named after the winged messenger in Greek Mythology. It is a radio beam transmitter of sorts. Pure brilliance and quite a strategic weapon…Work of the best brains in Germany and Japan. You can send messages to the other side of the earth with minimum effort."

The Air Corps captain is just in awe over the device and its intended function.

"Most impressive, I doubt if they'll get that thing to work…"

The Dutchman is quite optimistic over his Axis comrades and comments further, "My dear Captain, you seriously underestimate the Third Reich's potential. One of the engineers also related to me the secret work going on in *Deutschland* (Germany) as we speak, with the development of rockets and the manipulation of the atom, and something called a jet plane without propellers. With the weapons of science, they will most certainly win this war. I stake my reputation on it. The Axis get to use my island for their experiments, and I don't mind their protection."

The Stockade

Ed Layton is eventually returned to the prisoner compound with its solitary hut and is reunited with the rest of his crew. Sergeant Komorowski meticulously cleans the last bit of rice from his plate to quell his hunger. Layton quietly briefs them on the entire meeting with the baron and the Germans. During the evening he paces back and forth along the guarded wire fence, reflecting on the grave situation. The sun is setting on the ocean in vivid splendor.

Lieutenant Foster gets two sips of water from the barrel and begins to question his pilot about the day's safari with the ruthless Dutch narcotics trafficker. "Boy, you managed to get a bit of sight-seeing in today didn't you? That German radio gizmo you told us about sounds like something out of Flash Gordon. Do you think it will work?" Ed Layton sits on a nearby bench and contemplates his answer.

"Probably. If they get that thing up and running, they can talk to their forces over great distances. Our navy intelligence guys would probably drool to get their hands on something like this. Maybe we can give them a hand. Somehow we have to send out a message of our own...not long distance though." The pilot gets up from the bench and walks over to the barbed wire fence. "Lieutenant, there is one thing that keeps gnawing at my bones, and I have been thinking of it since we got here. Why hasn't this island been discovered by the Allies? These skies are always patrolled by long range aircraft." He kicks the sand briefly with his boot in frustration, "How could they miss this place?"

Baron Vandermeer is in his office, making entries into his account ledger, and clicking away on the keys of his adding machine. The short-wave radio crackles in the background as BBC World News broadcasts the latest coverage of the war in Europe. The face mask of an island headhunter hangs menacingly on the wall behind the baron's desk.

British Intelligence

The scene changes, showing the same mask now as a gold necklace, framed between a pair of well-defined breasts of an intelligence officer. Her name is Lieutenant Carol Loxley, a native of Southampton, England. Her father Alfred was heavily involved with the merchant marine and had a sailboat. He taught his daughter the skills of sailing, geography, and cryptology. Her father and Carl Vandermeer have been business associates since long before the war started.

Alfred's enterprising daughter is assigned to the Far East Asian section of British intelligence located in Port Moresby, New Guinea. She is a photo interpreter and serves as liaison between the British and Allied military intelligence forces in the South Pacific. Her analysis of aerial photography is then passed on to aerial reconnaissance and bombing groups in the area. She is in a crucial position. Little does anyone realize that this outstanding W.A.A.F. (Women's Auxillary Air Force) officer, code-named 'The Raven' by the baron, is actually on the drug trafficker's payroll earning several thousand pounds a year, held in a private Swiss bank account. Her main job, in the eyes of the narcotics kingpin, is to keep the Allies away from his facilities as long as possible in order to maintain his flourishing opium trade. She is stunningly attractive and fills the uniform well, turning the eyes of many male personnel.

Despite her somewhat cheerful demeanor, the woman quietly mourns over the loss of her husband, who met his untimely end in a plane crash in England earlier in the year.

One fine morning in the operations room, she receives notice that two American Navy flying boats are going to be dispatched from their airfields on newly liberated islands in the Solomons. They are to proceed northward to search for any signs of Japanese shipping. Her beautiful eyes carefully glance over the map, making sure that no Allied aircraft will pass on or near the baron's island. The reconnaissance sweeps are set up in her office, utilizing Carol's latest evaluation of incoming aerial photographs. Her findings are submitted to her boss, air operations officer Major Samantha Clark, who in turn notifies reconnaissance squadrons in the affected areas. The photographic division is run by General Michael Kingston. Loxley's eyes carefully glide over the map on operations room wall and paperwork on the desks as she strolls about the center. The traitorous woman then gently unlocks her powers of persuasion to manipulate air operations with great poise and elegance. She enters an office.

"Major, what are the latest reported positions of TANGO 7 and 8? They had left the Solomons this morning. Any word yet from the Americans as far as their present patrol positions?" Lieutenant Loxley inquires. In the room with Major Clark is the female teenager, Corporal Cynthia Moneypenny, her unofficial *aide de camp*. Clark motions for the corporal to get the clipboard with the latest radio reports. The information is handed over, and the operations officer glances at the data. "TANGO 7, last reported in 10 minutes ago, position 3 degrees South, 157 degrees East, heading towards Nauru Island. TANGO 8 is at 6 degrees South, 149 degrees East, holding a course south of Arawe, New Britain.

One of the long-range PBY Catalina floatplanes is dangerously close to the baron's island. The reason for the flight is quite obvious. Japanese naval forces might attempt to out-flank Admiral Halsey's fleet in the Solomons. Carol gently traces the flight of one of the aircraft on the wall map. The course of the finger runs northward toward Nauru Island and makes her somewhat uncomfortable. It is in the vicinity of the Baron's enclave. However, the quick-thinking lieutenant directs the major to move the aircraft toward a position clear of storm-battered Bougainville to check for the remnants of the latest supply convoy hit by American medium bombers.

If there are a number of ships still afloat, it might warrant a new strike by the Americans.

The lieutenant comments, "Major Clark, I would like to suggest that we alter the course of TANGO 7, more to the southeast. I suspect that the Japanese may attempt another delivery of supplies to Empress Augusta Bay in wake of that bloody storm."

The major then studies the suggested course correction beside the top photo interpreter in the Royal Air Force at the wall map. Clark glances into the beautiful eyes of the recon expert. "Lieutenant, that is very possible. The Japanese are quite persistent in their logistics. We have heard that they were given a damn good thrashing yesterday, just like their raid in March. Nonetheless, I agree, and they will try and send more convoys. What course change do you recommend?"

The photo expert recommends the following: "I would suggest a new course of roughly 3 degrees South, 155 degrees East, on a heading 270 degrees due East toward Nuguria Island, and then on to Feni Island at 4 degrees South, 154 degrees East, on a heading 260 degrees Southeast."

The major glances at the map and has Carol annotate the new course heading on the radio intercept sheet. "Corporal!"

The young woman steps forward, "Yes Major?"

The clipboard is handed over as the major replies, "Be a dear and pass these new coordinates to TANGO 7 immediately. Off to the radio room you go." The corporal acknowledges and exits the room. Lieutenant Loxley then turns and begins to leave the office and walk back to her cluttered desk, followed by Samantha, who is very concerned with Carol's workload.

"You know Lieutenant... Carol. I have seen you working day and night." They both stop at Carol's desk. "Seemingly without rest, why, since you have lost your husband. Are you pushing yourself to the edge out here? To an early grave? Why not go back to England and be with family? I can have General Kingston issue you leave or have you transferred for God's sake!"

Carol is taken aback by the last sentence. She appears distressed and refuses the offer and begins her passionate plea to remain at her post, always being an expert in the art of manipulation. The lieutenant turns on her mesmerizing eyes to cast a slight spell on Major Clark and moves her to change her mind, like with the course of the reconnaissance aircraft minutes previously. "Major, please don't send me back. I want to stay in the middle of the action here. Not back to the fog and the rain. Please don't. I just can't sit and grieve the loss of my husband, soaking one bloody handkerchief after another. I need to stay busy, not being a Hob Knob though! Look at all these photographs yet to be analyzed."

Major Clark then smiles and gives a warm pat on Loxley's shoulder and consoles her, "All right, I withdraw the request for you to return home. The sense of loss you are struggling with....I don't envy being in your shoes. I haven't seen my husband Harold in six months. I don't know what I would do without him. This war is hell on relationships. Whereas your husband risked his life testing our most advanced aircraft, mine is outside London serving in the Godforsaken Barrage Balloon Corps!" The women then share laughs among themselves.

Joining the group of intelligence personnel in the operations room with Lieutenant Loxley is Sergeant Major Walter Baldwin, the rather whimsical records staff assistant. He is a newcomer to the Pacific War, being on his first tour of duty, and is infatuated with Carol, his charming coworker. Baldwin enters the operations room with a tray full of fresh coffee and cups. Carol then sits at her desk to resume her interpretation work of aerial reconnaissance photos. She takes the magnifier in hand and wants to begin her work. Major Clark watches the interpreter do her photographic wizardry. Corporal Moneypenny suddenly appears to drop a small packet of fresh aerial photographs on her desk and walks off. The sergeant major enters the immediate vicinity. "Ladies, would either of you care for a bit of coffee?"

The major accepts with pleasure. 'Thank you sergeant major, I'd be delighted."

Baldwin continues his splendid accommodation. "I also have cream and sugar." The soldier then turns to set his eyes on Lieutenant Loxley, "Lieutenant? Would you like a cup?"

Carol then gives the sergeant a stern look with beady eyes, and flexing her jaw, a thoroughly well-broadcasted, "No!" He clears his throat and then is soon off to the other side of the room. His good friend Corporal Moneypenny is at a file cabinet and wants to stop by for a brief chat.

"Care for some coffee corporal?" The girl accepts with pleasure and remarks, "Yes, I'd be delighted." She then whispers, "How are things with the lieutenant coming along?"

The sergeant major looks around to make sure no one listens in on the delicate conversation. "Well Penny, I tried to give her a cup of coffee and she almost bit my bloody head off!"

The corporal whispers back, "Well give it time. I can see it in her eyes, she does like you. Who knows, maybe cupid's arrow will strike her soon enough."

Baldwin commented, "Don't be daft! How can you tell?"

The girl answers, "Well, I have been following Loxley and the plight of her husband. It is bollocks that she loved him that much. There have been rumors of the pilot's affair with another woman at the aircraft test center. I am not sure about it … but I have heard some rumors."

The sergeant replies, "You mean?"

"Yes," the girl answers. The sergeant is now under the misimpression that Carol has a bit of a crush on him. Moneypenny meant the rumors of marital misconduct may be true.

The Challenge

It is early morning as Japanese soldiers arrive to usher the crew out of the bamboo cage and into an army truck. Lieutenant Foster remarks, "Captain, this better not be the final round up!" The men are driven, under guard, to a rice paddy field where they are given hand tools and forced to begin their labor. The rising sun is seen on the horizon—an absolutely beautiful sight. The men wade into the field and work along with several natives, harvesting rice at gunpoint. When the guards speak among themselves, Argendizo turns his back on them and imitates the Japanese with big buckteeth and squinted eyes. His improvisation generates smiles amongst his fellow laborers. The army scout car arrives at the rice field carrying Carl and Col. Yakashi. The prisoners start to work in the field. The baron tells Yakashi, "Colonel, please have your chaps bring the American pilot over here. Thank you." A soldier goes way out into the field to pick up the prisoner.

Randy wades into the water and remarks to a local native, "Nothing like getting trench foot in this slimy goop!"

George and Jerry work in the field together and carry on a light conversation. "There is one thing to be grateful for working this early in the morning. If they hauled us out here in the afternoon, we'd be dead of heat stroke," Jerry commented. "Hey, whatever it takes to save bullets, it could be their plan. It sounds reasonable enough. As long as there aren't any leeches or poisonous snakes in this muck!" Jerry adds with a touch of sarcasm. The Chicago native then looks around his feet with a sense of fear. Komorowski continues, "I wish we could do this with a tractor. My dad works in the stockyards of Chicago. Boy, he'd be proud of me. I am the eldest of four sons." Argendizo offers a smile in acknowledgement as George continues. "He came from Krakow."

Lieutenant Foster stops working briefly to catch his breath. A native comes up to help him in his section of the field. Foster tries to keep his sense of humor and strikes up a conversation with the local, who understands no English whatsoever. "It is amazing how you guys can do this rice stuff all day long. I bet you don't get paid a cent for it. You guys need to form a labor union more than anything else! Hey, after all, it's the American Way." The man smiles at him. The native then shows the copilot a specific harvesting technique, and Randy humorously tries to imitate the stroke of the hand tool. A distance away, a Japanese soldier is keeping his eye on the airman.

The copilot then whistles to himself a familiar American melody, "I've Been Working on the Railroad." The amateur crooner starts to sing the song, with much amusement of his fellow workers. "I've been working on the railroad, all the live long day... I've been working in the rice field just to pass the time away..." The copilot then pauses, his face now gripped with anger. He then continues singing but now thrashing the hand tool violently to wreck the crop. "Can't you hear the whistle blowing, Rising Sun, early in the 'morn. Can't you hear the colonel shouting?!"

A Japanese soldier suddenly comes up on the copilot and shouts at him to stop singing and destroying the rice crop. A rifle is pointed and contact is made with Randy's torso. The native worker runs away with fright. The lieutenant drops his tool in an act of defiance. The soldier is fuming, enraged at the disobedience, and points the rifle at the tool and motions for the American to start working. Randy then puts his hands up, motioning that he meant no harm, with a goofy smile. Tex replies with a smirk, "Whoa Nelly! I was just having a bit of fun!" and then reaches down to pick up his tool. The soldier then shouts, "Work!" and then storms off. He is greeted by another guard and inquires what went wrong. "Saburo! What happened?"

The frustrated soldier then replies, thumbing, "Another guy who thinks he's Frank Sinatra!"

Captain Layton has left the rice paddy and makes his way to the scout car under guard. Colonel Yakashi then motions for the soldier to leave. The baron begins his discussion with the American pilot. "Good Morning Captain. I hope that you and your crew rested peacefully once again. I'd been doing some thinking last night. What a shame it would be to have the manpower such as your crew, languishing in the fields till war's end."

Layton does not take the matter lying down and remarks, "You know it's against the Geneva Convention to use prisoners for forced labor."

The baron shares a brief chuckle with Colonel Yakashi and replies, "Now Mr. Layton, it's not too arduous to harvest a bit of rice now, is it? Hardly backbreaking. Maybe your labor could be put to better use, let's say, helping in running my narcotics operation. I could promise you better food, oh definitely better, and pay your crew double their salary."

The pilot steadfastly refuses the offer. He motions with his head and says, "I am very sorry baron. I have no intention of letting my surviving men languish on this island longer than they have to." He continued as a look of sincere disappointment grips Vandermeer's face. The baron's hopes for a suitable and above all, intelligent, business partner, have most certainly been dashed. "Soon this island will be discovered by some of our aircraft, and we'll be rescued and *you* sir, will be locked up in the ship's brig! You are nothing but a two-bit crook."

The baron now slumps in the car seat and looks at Yakashi sitting next to him. He gathers his thoughts. "Your pompous confidence is nauseating. Here I thought you would be reasonable!" Layton listens intently. "An intelligent man would accept my offer to care for the safety of his crew. I often wonder how soldiers like yourselves stay loyal to the cause of war after being enlightened to the truth."

The American now fires a broadside. "Don't look at me! My country did-n't start it. Just ask Colonel Yakashi here, he'll tell you about what happened in Hawaii… Pearl Harbor is nice this time of year. Go and see the charred hulk of the battleship Arizona. Have a picnic, what the hell!"

The colonel is irritated by the outburst. "Captain. I can have the firing squad ready in minutes, or better yet, I can have you and your men sent off to Siam. We need a railway bridge completed. The British are there now and you can join them."

The baron quickly jumps into the conversation, "Colonel, please let me have him to…"

Yakashi replied, "Okay…Either way he is going to die."

The pilot fires back once again. "I'm sorry if you take offense to my re-action. I am just allergic to Axis collaboration, that's all. I break out in a rash at the thought of it, but for yourself, being a civilian, umm…ruthless busi-nessman, I don't blame you for your line of reasoning. On this island I would say you are insulated from reality."

The baron takes offense to the last remark. Once more the American's word blows another hole through the Dutchman's ego. Carl will not take any jibes sitting down. "Reality, okay…Very well Captain, you leave me no choice. Enough of your arrogance and my hospitality. Back in my study I told you about a new animal that I've created to hunt."

Layton replies "Yes, I'm curious baron, what characteristics does this *thing* have? What must it be able to do?"

The baron replies, "Well, it must have courage, be daring, cunning and above all… it must have the ability to reason."

Layton probes deeper, "But no animal can reason." There is silence in the scout car. A devious smile appears on Carl's face, and he gives the pilot a cold stare. He remarks, "This is one that can." The captain ponders the state-ment, and it dawns on him, that *he* is the wild game! He then reacts. "This has to be some kind of morbid joke…What you are talking about has nothing to do with hunting… but murder!" The baron's face is gripped with irritation, and he retaliates. "Oh come now Captain. You and your men fly an aircraft, bomb and strafe targets, kill Japs as you call them, and you have the audacity to question me on the value of human life!"

Layton angrily fires back "I'm a pilot, not a murderer! There is a difference. This is murder!" "No," Carl replies, "Not murder, but an experiment! I would like to measure the performance of humans in the wild, away from their concrete jungles, with people scurrying back and forth to work each day. I find it amusing to watch humans like yourselves as they try to adapt to nature like that found on this desolate island. After periods of observation..."

Layton interjects. "Through a rifle scope and measurement."

Carl continued, "I formulate a hypothesis and conclusion to the human survival instinct." Carl continues. "How do they survive and cope? No animal can survive against me. That is a statistical fact. I get a thrill out of watching men break down in the elements. 'Survival of the fittest,' Darwin once said. Now there's a real genius!" Colonel Yakashi exits the car and walks over to his soldiers and checks on the rice harvest. The crewmen of *Bugs Bunny* keep their focus on the intense discussion in the scout car.

Captain Layton takes the podium. "Now you are a naturalist, and let me guess, your rifle is a "scientific tool" used to …. test the reflexes and stamina of the specimen in the wild, which is me."

The Dutchman is simply delighted. "Precisely my boy! You're catching on quickly with your ability to reason. This is an island yes, and it has its boundaries, and you're not going anywhere."

The pilot quietly mutters to himself, "I'm a lousy swimmer…"

The Dutchman pounces, "What's that? Oh you are…I will make note of that in my journal?" Ed regrets the last remark.

"Against sharks, what difference would it make," Layton comments.

"I offer you this, Mr. Layton. Tomorrow at sunrise I will hunt you down in my jungle, and if you can survive and reach the altar of the old missionary school on the other side of the island, you will bow down and ask for salvation and mercy. I will then release you and your crew back to New Guinea unharmed. I have an extra motor launch to get you on your way Captain. I mean it!"

Layton thinks it over and questions, "What about the colonel? He isn't simply going to watch us, castaways, simply escape!"

Carl replies, "I have considerable sway with the colonel. Remember about my wealth and buying influence in foreign governments. Look at it this way..."

The pilot interjects, "I get it, the colonel is on your payroll."

The baron quickly continued, "Yes! Allow me to finish...I consider this to be what you Americans call a children's game of hide and go seek...you hide...and I seek. If I catch you in my scope, you will not leave the jungle alive. It pits your instinct for survival against my superior marksmanship. If you choose to decline Mr. Layton, you and your men will be handed over to the colonel. I will not be responsible for his actions. He lost his sister during Doolittle's bombing raid on Nagoya, Japan after your country entered the war." Layton reflects on the similarity of the aircraft used in the raid and his own. "He is not feeling very ... charitable, and your lives will become written history. Cooperate with me, and, by some slim hope, survive my game, and I give you my word the colonel will not touch your men. I have been protecting you all this time. Don't lose sight of that. When you go back to the States, you can be a big hero like in the movies. Gary Cooper will have met his match. Think it over."

Layton pauses for a moment, reflects on the situation and replies, "I accept the challenge, if it secures the release of my crew."

"Excellent!" replies Vandermeer with a smile. "I should hope so...My men will collect you shortly before sunrise, and I will double your crews' food rations from this very moment. Have a good, restful evening Mr. Layton...You're going to need it in the morning."

The pilot comments for the last time before parting, "Well, seeing that I'll soon be standing in the Valley of the Shadow of Death, baron... Curiosity is eating me alive. I've got to hand it to you, how you've been able to escape detection from our forces all this time. It amazes me. Obviously, your past safaris have taught you well the value of camouflage. Tell me, how did you do it? Surely *somebody's* got to know you're out here."

Carl pauses. He replies. "Captain, let me tell you a story."

Layton mutters under his brow, "Here we go again!"

"During the First World War, a German auxiliary cruiser, the S.M.S. Wolf (readers shall reference *The Cruise of the Raider Wolf* by Roy Alexander) used to roam these waters off Rabaul disguised as an innocent freighter in search of enemy shipping. With every ship captured through complete surprise, the captain took whole crews aboard and kept them under lock and key to prevent any news of his ship's presence in the area leaking out and alerting the Admiralty. Each captured ship was stripped of useful cargo and sunk. One crafty prisoner aboard the raider decided to throw bottles overboard containing distress messages with the hope that someone would find them. The Admiralty did receive the messages, only weeks later, and by that time the German ship was safely out of reach.

I did manage to get a hold of one of these bottles years later. It sits in my office, a stark reminder, showing the importance of controlling information. Whoever controls the flow of information can deceive the enemy by manipulating the variables and circumstances, either externally or from within, like I do. That is why I remain elusive to this day.

Whereas the *Wolf* had an eye in the sky in the form of a scout plane to protect the phantom ship, I have eyes of my own. What beautiful ones they are, working and watching over me, to protect me from those same Allies nearly thirty years later. Controlling the information my boy, that's the key. The ship covered up its wake each time and was never caught, and returned to Germany triumphantly in 1918. I shall do the same, leave no tracks, no stone unturned, no wake. Unlike the *Wolf*, which harbored several hundred prisoners below decks, I have the luxury of holding only your aircrew."

The captain is amazed by the Dutchman's vast knowledge, "How did you find out about all this stuff?"

The baron replies sternly, "I read books!" Layton returns to his men behind the barbed wire later in the afternoon. The aircrew is exhausted after their first day of toiling in the fields at gunpoint with repeated altercations with the guards.

Confrontation

At sunset the pilot again briefs the men in the hut as to the deal he struck with the notorious narcotics trafficker.

"Are you outta your cotton pickin' mind? You don't know what awaits you out there!" shouts Lieutenant Foster. "While you and Mister Van der whatever are carrying out your little *business discussion*, we're out in the fields harvestin' damn rice...I hate rice Ed! Let me tell you something...that jungle is as thick as a cornfield, and sharp as a knife. I'd like to see you run through the sharp elephant grass. It's nice to see you lay down your carcass for us, but you don't got a chance. We'll never get out of this place...It's too heavily guarded." He turns his head, looking out the hut window at the barbed wire. The guards menacingly pace back and forth. The Japanese do take notice of the impending heated discussion behind the barbed wire enclosure.

"I take it you don't like my idea. It may have a chance to save all of us, don't you understand?" Layton replies.

His copilot quickly answers with irritation. "I think it stinks personally, just one step closer to collaboration in my book. The food is lousy, and now we're going to be getting twice as much. Brilliant."

The pilot burns with anger. "Collaborating... That's a bunch of bull crap... I..."

Foster retaliates, "How can you trust this guy? When you leave tomorrow morning, you'll be dead by noon, and then the baron will come back and have the colonel shoot all of us... plain and simple! You know, us country folk aren't that damn stupid, and I don't think you have the street smarts either!"

Layton approaches the copilot almost nose to nose. "You're just jealous because I made captain before you did, aren't you?" Hatred fills Randy's eyes. "Now I think I hit a raw nerve, didn't I! You think I broke under pressure? I didn't... kept us all from turning out to be Spam in a can on crash landing." Foster starts to smolder in anger as the aircrewmen watch the unfolding argument with disbelief. He shouts, "I'm not in this war for a medal captain, just to learn how to stay alive! I wasn't at Midway, and now I wonder what really did happen that day... Tell me Sir, did you see any ships? Huh? Did you see any?! I'm living with a bag of luck from Texas, and what do you have?" The copilot feels for his missing Air Corps pilot wings, confiscated by a Jap soldier the previous day. "I can see you in the cross hairs now. "Pop! One prairie dog less! Ego hasn't a chance against bullets..." A Japanese soldier smiles with amusement as the quarrel behind the bamboo intensifies and then turns around to get a drink of water from a nearby water barrel.

In the prison hut, a knife flies across the room and lands on the post between the two startled pilots. "That's far enough guys. Break it up," remarks Jerry Argendizo. "I got an idea." He motions for the men to gather. "Captain, while you're getting chased, it could give us an excellent opportunity to escape. The Japs will be distracted and eager to watch the safari festivities."

"Nope," Lieutenant Foster interrupts. "We're too heavily guarded. Maybe we should ask Harry Houdini on how to get out of here. Remember the old R.A.F. uniform that George found? Some died trying."

The newsman continues, "Lieutenant, let me finish. We can ditch these Japs and rendezvous at the dock area. They have some pretty nice boats stashed away there. The jungle will give us a great place to hide and await your return, provided you survive the hunt. I'd like to get into the radio hut and send out a message to the fleet to let them know where we are. Intelligence always picks up these things, they have ears… It's worth a try." Komorowski issues his warning. "Lt. Foster might be right. They might all come back and shoot all of us. We can at least try, instead of sitting around on our *dupas,*" (Polish term meaning rear end).

The crewmen muse over the proposal and accept the idea. Jerry then suggests, "We need a diversion to draw the guards in here so we can knock the daylights out of them. We need to create some noise, an explosion, set off some fireworks. Who knows, the smoke from the island may be an effective smoke signal to our passing planes. This would give me enough time to get out a quick message. I saw the radio hut and weenie behind the receiver. I can take him with my knife!'

"Don't worry," remarks Sergeant Komorowski." Daryl and I will also think of something to get rid of the guards. After we break out, we're heading for the boats and going to hold one for our cruise. We'll wait for you guys at the dock if any of you care to join us. We will cast off at noon." The copilot still remains skeptical about a successful escape.

"Well, let's do it. If we stay here any longer, we all might end up being shot. Lieutenant, I agree with you after thinking it over," Layton remarked. "I'll be getting chased from one side of this island to the other by that nut, and you guys make a break for it. We will meet at the dock. If I am late, by all means take off without me! Clear!"

Komorowski interjects, "We'll break out after they feed us in the morning so we at least have some energy. Captain, may God protect you in the jungle." The sergeant then makes the sign of the cross and then explains his plan to the New Yorker. "Now Jerry, here's what's going to happen. Daryl you and I…" The men decide to put their plan into action and wish their captain the best of luck as they turn in for the night. A single guard circles the compound calmly smoking his cigarette. The jungle is quiet and in total darkness.

Within two hours, the silence of the jungle is broken by the sounds of soldiers singing a Japanese funeral song at a distant campfire. The faces of the soldiers are cast in an eerie light by the flickering flames of the fire.

"Umi yukaba mizuku kabana. Yama yukaba mizuku kabana. Yame yu-kaba kusamasu kabana. Ookimi no henikoso shiname. Karimiwa seji."

Layton and Foster peer out from the hut window. Jerry gets up from his bed and joins the men and then says, "What is that? That singing sounds creepy. Did someone kick the bucket?"

The rest of the aircrew gathered near the window to hear the eerie sound. Layton remarks, "I feel really strange... It's like a specter of death has gotten a hold of this place."

"The Grim Reaper," Argendizo interjects.

Foster then tries to reassure the guys, "It's probably being done deliberately and just fooling with our nerves Captain. I wouldn't worry too much about it." The copilot then returns to his bunk.

The newsman then has a quiet last word with the pilot. "You know Captain. I gotta hand it to you, sacrificing your life to try to get us all free. I bet you can take on this Dutch guy and win this most dangerous game."

Layton then pats the shoulder of his colleague and remarks, "A game the baron wants, a game he will get!"

The Chess Match

One lone light pierces the darkness of the baron's lair. Carl Vandermeer and the colonel engage in a gentleman's game of chess as the phonograph plays classical music behind them. The men sip on imported wine. "I see, Colonel that you are on top of your game this evening. You have beaten me previously, and I haven't forgotten. However, tonight I have calculated your every move and countermove."

Carl maneuvers his queen into a strategic position and remarks, "Check mate!" The Japanese colonel is surprised, analyzes the last moves, and admits defeat.

"Brilliant," he remarks. "I'll be ready for you tomorrow in our next game, after you finish off the American pilot."

A sudden knock on the door interrupts the light atmosphere. The colonel stands up and opens the door. Outside is a Japanese sergeant, who relays the depressing news that Admiral Yamamoto perished in a plane crash near Rabaul earlier in the day. The fateful radio broadcast had been heard. Yakashi then briefs the baron about the loss of the admiral. "It seems that Admiral Yamamoto perished in a plane crash this afternoon. He was an excellent tactician, who planned the raid at Pearl Harbor, even though he had death threats against him. He even opposed any alliance with Nazi Germany. I liked him personally... a great loss for our country."

The Japanese colonel then begins to ponder his future. "I have some news of my own. At the end of this month, you're going to have to find a new chess partner. Maybe my adjutant can take over. I'm going to be transferred to army headquarters in the Philippines with a promotion. I had received this message over the radio from Rabaul earlier today."

The baron is moved by the news and promptly reaches for the wine bottle to refill the glasses. He then replies with a sense of admiration. "That's great news! I'm sure they chose the best man for the job. Now, a toast to the new assignment and your new promotion. In the passing of Yamamoto, new opportunities will arise. Count on it."

The army officer drinks more wine and then comments with remorse, "I was hoping to return to Japan and my family and enjoy a quiet retirement. I guess things are not running very well for us in this war. I don't want to work on Yamashita's hectic army staff, our 'Tiger of Malaya.'"

Yakashi then questions the narcotics kingpin. "Will you be ready for the challenge with the American captain in the morning? He is very strong...I can feel it, especially after we captured him. He is unlike the others you've..."

The baron interrupts "Captain Layton, as you perceive correctly, is very strong. He has a complex personality I have yet to figure out. I've seen the others break a lot sooner than he. Tomorrow we will find out." Vandermeer then reaches for the colonel's king chess piece and places it in the palm of his hand. "I will find a way to break the American." The anger pouring through his veins incites him to crush the game piece before the colonel's eyes.

"Then, Colonel Yakashi, there are the others... I despise the Texan... He's next." Carl reaches for the horseman chess piece and puts it in his hand. "A pompous cowboy... he won't leave my O.K. Corral after I put a bullet in his head!" He crushes the horse figurine in a similar fashion. "Alas, then we have the altar boy from Chicago (picks up the bishop game piece). Not even God can spare him the fate that awaits him in this tropical 'purgatory.'" The baron inverts the bishop with its symbolic cross and angrily imbeds it into the chess table into a virtual pile of dust. "You see... Ashes to ashes, dust to dust." He then blows the remains off the table.

The Hunt Begins

Jerry is up early with the rising sun once again and silently dictates another mental letter to his mother.

> *"Dear Mom: I have no paper or pencil to write with, but I hope you get my mental note. The last mission we flew ended in a complete mess. We crash landed on an island after a bad storm and sank some Jap ships. We're being held prisoner by a ruthless drug trafficker and evil Japanese Colonel. It is a miracle (Hail Mary!) that we were not executed by a firing squad when we got caught. I know that I am a journalist, a non-combatant of sorts, but I just can't take things sitting down. I will fight! Today is our big day, "Redemption Day." We are going to attempt the biggest escape from our tropical prison. Guess how? Our Captain, Ed Layton has accepted a wild jungle challenge. He bet the Dutch Baron that he can survive a jungle hunt, unarmed, and survive a wild chase to the other side of the island. Get this! If he survives the hunt, we will all be set free! Sounds crazy, but heck, it's worth a try. While this safari is going on, we have a plan to bust on outta here. God be with*

us, because if anything goes wrong, and our timing is a little off, I will be playing a harp. Talk to you soon. I love you, Your Bambino. P.S. Don't send any cookies, the Nazis and the Punjab will eat them all!"

The men had slept for several hours as the sound of soldiers approach in the darkness. The gate creaks open at daybreak as the Japanese colonel enters the compound. Layton stands up from his bed and is quietly led away. His colleagues are speechless and stare out the window. George makes the sign of the cross. The pilot is taken under guard to a truck and speeds off in the direction of the rice paddies. The sun begins its slow ascent on the horizon into a fiery pink sky. From his seat, Layton sees horses, a dozen natives, and a few Japanese soldiers. The truck stops on the bumpy, unforgiving road to deliver Layton to his early morning appointment with certain death.

"Good Morning Mr. Layton," as Baron Vandermeer extends his hand awaiting a gentlemen's handshake. Ed refuses with a cold stare. A Japanese soldier angrily pushes Ed behind the back for his apparent lack of respect. Carl motions with his hands, "It's nothing, ignore it."

The Dutchman is fully dressed in his tropical hunting gear, with his superb hunting rifle slung over his shoulder. He is on his impressive horse and says, "Well, Mr. Layton, your time has now come, when your apparent silence will soon... How shall we say it... match that of the jungle. Observe ... your last sunrise, what a beautiful one it is indeed." Layton is unmoved by the statement and calmly yawns. The Dutchman then offers the pilot a knife and remarks, "Here...you'll need this to cut through what awaits you out there." The captain stares at the seemingly useless small knife just handed to him.

Vandermeer then cycles the bolt of his rifle back and forth once. "Since I'm a man of honor and a man of my word, I will now give you a ten minute head start. Now...have you any last requests before you expire, excuse me, perspire. Like water perhaps?" A Japanese soldier then steps forward with a water canteen and offers it with a slight bow. *"Nanika nomimono-wa ikaga desuka?"* (May I offer you something to drink?) Layton takes the canteen with its belt and drapes it over his shoulder.

"Now Captain, let me direct you to the path of your destiny (clumsily pointing). It's that way!" His hand points to the dense tropical forest. The pilot then begins his lonely trek into the wet fields, pauses, and then turns toward Carl and smiles. He darts across the field into the underbrush and disappears. The baron then adjusts his seat in the saddle aboard his horse, staring at his watch. The natives grow restless, eager to give chase. However, the hunter restrains them. The Japanese soldiers visually follow the flight of the American, staring into the jungle. The reflection of the pilot running to the jungle reflects on the lenses of the intrepid hunter's glasses.

The Escape

Inside the bamboo stockade, the surviving members of *Bugs Bunny* try to stomach the extra portion of dry rice cakes and water they got for breakfast. Randy shakes his head with disgust at his food. "I think I can't take one more day of this slop. Man cannot live on rice alone. I wish I was home and sitting at the breakfast table with oatmeal, toast, eggs, and bacon."

The four men leave the hut under the watchful eye of the guard and then walk around the wire enclosure as they put their plan into action. Moments later, Daryl Ford complains of stomach pains. "Guys, I feel sick. Maybe I ate damn infected larvae or something! My stomach is just killing me." The top turret gunner then hunches over a bit holding his stomach. Sergeant Komorowski quickly comes over to him, apparently thinking that the airman is joking.

"Daryl, what's up? Having trouble?"

Ford looks up at his faithful comrade and flippantly replies, "It was the rice I ate, you meathead! The water they cooked it in must have been bad. I have stomach cramps, and I am going to blow chow! It hurts, help me!" The airman then collapses to the ground withering in pain. Jerry starts to laugh and jeer.

The copilot then steps forward and stands above the gunner. He begins to shout, "Oh come on Daryl, knock it off. Quit clowning around! Get back on your feet sergeant!" George stands ready with Tex to knock out the guard as Jerry shouts from the fence and motions to the guard to come and render aid. The soldier watches silently, apparently unmoved by the words or motions of the group... calmly lighting another cigarette and lazily blowing the smoke into the air.

Daryl begins to choke violently, evenly intentionally biting his lip to make the situation worse than it seemed. Jerry yells out to the soldier, "For Christ's sake can't you see the guy's bleeding! He's in pain! Come in here and help us. Don't just stand there and watch this guy suffer!" He redoubles his efforts to draw the guard forward, without success. After another moment of hesitation, the Japanese soldier finally moves to the gate, as the Americans anxiously await his entrance. The guard then stops in front of the barbed wire gate, hesitates, and then reaches into his pocket. It looks like everything is running smoothly as planned. A key will soon be forthcoming, and the guard will be overpowered. However, the soldier pulls out a whistle and promptly blows on it for several seconds.

The Americans exchange bewildered looks as their plan may have gone awry. The men utter words of great disappointment. Within seconds, three armed foot soldiers arrive, and then the gate is opened. The prisoners are very disappointed. Japanese soldiers, with their Ariska rifles drawn, guard Jerry, Randy, and George as the remaining soldier prods his rifle at Ford, attempting to roll him over. The soldier mutters, *"Ima kore kara?"* (What now?) Daryl continues to scream aloud. He grabs his stomach as the Japanese turn away from the other airmen to observe the commotion. The Japanese guard gets too close as Ford takes out his legs with a swift kick. Within seconds all of the guards are rendered unconscious. The men quietly dart from their cage with an eventual rendezvous at the motor launch. Foster stuffs a Nambu pistol and two grenades in his uniform while the others carry the rifles. He also recovers his coveted air corps wing badge from the body of a soldier and remarks "Next time ask!" Randy then notifies his fellow airman that he had a score to settle with Colonel Yakashi. The copilot disappears into the jungle amid the protests of his colleagues.

The Jungle Adventure

As the hands of his watch show ten minutes past, Vandermeer lets out a shout. "All right men. Let's move out!" and signals with his hands that the hunt will now begin. The two horses carrying Carl and a native scout gallop across the rice paddy toward the jungle. The natives follow, armed with clubs and sticks, yelling a tribal hunting song.

Layton is running as quickly as possible, navigating thick mud bogs and dense underbrush. Cuts appear on his forearms as he sweeps aside the dense, sharp elephant grass. He notices that some of his blood is on the grass itself. He wipes the sweat from his head and continues through the grass. Carl Vandermeer's hunting party now enters the jungle and tracks the trail of foot prints before him. The Dutchman smiles with delight, as tracking the elusive human specimen will be relatively easy.

Several hundred yards distant, the pilot pauses to catch his breath beside a palm tree after several minutes of running. Little does he realize that a poisonous snake silently glides down the tree trunk toward his head. It eventually shows its ugly, slender head and black tongue right in front of the exhausted captain's face. He instinctively grabs the snake's head with a yell and rams it into the tree trunk. The snake dies instantly, with Layton hyperventilating with fear. He manages to catch his breath and continue onward through the dense jungle. His hands move the bushes aside with every stride. One moment, something catches his eye. What is it? He notices something lying in the underbrush. Moving leaves aside, he carefully reaches for a dark object and discovers it to be a British army-issued combat boot. He pauses for a moment, wondering about its origin, and soon takes notice of the footprints left by his combat boots. Layton analyzes the situation and then strikes upon an idea. The look of despair on his face is replaced with a smile as he tosses the old combat boot aside. He then runs in several large circles across the jungle floor in an effort to confuse the baron. Ed pulls out his small knife and begins to cut off two large thick leaves from a bush. The crafty pilot then sits down on a tree trunk, unties his boots, wraps a leaf over the sole of each boot, and secures them with his shoelaces. Layton then walks several yards with his boots and notices the absence of any visible footprints.

The baron and faithful scout surge ahead through the jungle and pause after several minutes. Vandermeer's eyes spot a broken trail of bushes. He gets off his horse and carefully investigates the foliage, noting a sign of blood. His eyes suddenly scan the ground and find a trail of footprints in the soft earth. He smiles and remarks, "This is going to be easy." The natives arrive and quietly observe the Dutchman at his tracking work. Carl follows the footprints, rifle in hand, and soon realizes that he is walking in circles. The baron successfully tracks the footprints to a bush with leaves missing and studies the soil with frustration. No more tracks to follow. The airman had vanished into thin air. "Crafty little bugger isn't he!" The hunter acknowledges the increasing difficulty.

About one mile ahead of the baron, Layton reaches for his canteen and takes a sip of water. He notices another Komodo dragon lizard walking clumsily in the distance. The trek through the jungle continues. His eyes nervously scan all directions in an effort, without success, to catch a glimpse of the intrepid hunter. Instead, they manage to focus their attention on a very large object lying several yards ahead of him. He investigates.

In a small clearing lie the remains of a R.A.F. C-47 Dakota transport plane. Layton moves toward the aircraft, clearing away more dense bushes impeding his path. He reaches the rear fuselage, noting the R.A.F. insignia on the bullet-riddled tail. His hands run across the rear empennage, touching the large painted British roundel. The pilot eventually reaches the cargo door and opens it. The adventurer climbs inside to explore the darkened interior, finding nothing of value after a perfunctory inspection.

He steps out the door and walks away from the plane. Layton then stops in his tracks after spotting one of the baron's imported hunting targets in the form of male African lion! The animal has him in his sights as Layton runs back into the fuselage, slams the clumsy cargo door closed, and huddles inside the airplane. The hungry lion paces the plane's left wing root, staring at his lunch through the windows. The pilot taunts the lion, "Another one of the baron's hunting toys, eh! If you're still alive, it means that he must be a lousy shot. Good for me! There is nothing to fear but fear itself." The animal violently claws at a nearby window with a roar. Captain Layton moves forward and sticks out his tongue to taunt the animal and then moves toward the cockpit as the fuselage shifts suddenly to the side. To his horror, the rear cargo door unlatches and slides open. The lion hustles aft, enters the wreck, and moves up the aisle toward the terrified pilot in the darkened interior.

The captain runs into the cockpit, slamming the flimsy door behind him. The lion ruthlessly claws at the locked door in an effort to break in. Ed pivots himself in the cockpit and stares eye to eye with the second lion! He is perched atop the cockpit nose, staring at him from behind the broken cockpit windscreen! The animal roars and claws at the pilot. Layton, sweating profusely, cries out in desperation, "My God!" He glances at his small knife and doubts its size will have any affect on the lion. He then searches the abandoned cockpit and by chance discovers a loaded flare pistol. He cocks the gun and blasts the lion through the cockpit glass. The animal disappears in a bright flash. The captain reloads the flare gun and blasts the remaining shell right through the cabin door amid the violent scratching. He hears the animal exit the fuselage. After judging that the area is safe, he resumes his trek through the dense jungle, flare gun at his side.

After several minutes, he pauses to rest beside a tree, and he hears the sound of the baron's hunting party in the immediate vicinity. His eyes frantically scan the dark jungle as sweat rolls down his forehead in the tropical heat. He wipes his brow after finishing another gulp of water from the canteen. Within a split second a bullet ricochets just above his head as the sound of a gunshot echoes through the jungle. Several birds scramble for the air in fright. Ed scurries away, eyes filled with terror, heart and lungs pounding as the chase continues.

Layton frantically runs through the bushes as another bullet zips past. He scales a small pile of rocks to elude his pursuers and runs for several yards, constantly looking behind him. Ed manages to hurdle a fallen tree and then feels the ground underneath his feet suddenly give way, revealing a dreaded Burmese tiger trap. The captain falls in, narrowly missing the deadly sharp spikes protruding up from the earth. His head bumps into the skeletal remains of a man impaled on a large stake. The pilot is gripped with fear as he covers his hands to mask his scream. Trembling with fear, he quickly crawls to the wall of the pit, away from his new found companion. He scans the body of skeleton inside the tiger trap. He examines the uniform closely and sees the wings and embroidered Royal Air Force emblem. Layton sits for a moment and analyzes the ramifications of the dead British crewman lying before him. Obviously the poor bloke evaded the baron's previous hunt and lost his life in the process.

The pilot frantically attempts to climb out of the pit minutes later; however, the sound of the baron's voice forces him to reconsider. He sits in the darkness staring at the dead man once again. After waiting for the hunting party to leave the area, he exits the pit, using a tree limb to climb out to safety. He removes the large leaves from his boots. The American sacrifices detection for speed. The Wisconsin native's luck runs out as one of the natives in the baron's hunting party spots him in the distance and shouts an alarm. Vandermeer and his guide turn their horses around and gallop to the shouts of the natives, who motion them in the direction of the elusive captain.

Trapped

Layton runs as fast as he can through the underbrush eventually reaching a raging waterfall where he scales the rocks to cross a river. Another ricocheting bullet signals the presence of the intrepid hunter. The pilot turns his head in all directions to locate the source of the gunfire without, success. The baron dismounts his horse and stands several yards away, positioning his rifle for the next shot. Several natives head down to the waters edge in anticipation of collecting the dead pilot's body. The natives begin to shout and cheer for the final shot. The hunter centers the unlucky captain in the crosshairs of his rifle. Layton struggles to keep his grip on the rocks and slips as the next bullet obliterates his water canteen.

The pilot continues to search for a way to navigate the waterfall, without success. Another shot is fired as Layton slips, grabs for his chest, and plunges off the waterfall. The natives let out a shout of joy as the American disappears under the plume of water below. The captain is engulfed by the wall of water and is carried away by a swift undercurrent. The turbulence of the water rips the fatigue uniform shirt right off his lifeless body.

Carl lowers his rifle with satisfaction and heads down to the riverbank several yards distant. The natives scan the water in search of the elusive pilot. Two of them enter the river to search for the body. No luck. Vandermeer is concerned that he might have missed and cycles the bolt of his rifle, ejecting the last empty cartridge. A native then shouts out that he has found something in the river. Sure enough, he pulls Layton's blood-stained uniform shirt from the water! The Dutchman then examines the find and places his finger through an apparent bullet hole in the chest pocket fabric. Carl nods his head in acknowledgement and remarks, "Now to kill the rest."

The hunting party leaves the area, with Layton observing them from the river, hidden beneath weeds. The American had miraculously survived with a superficial chest wound. He then swims onward and eventually disappears into the jungle. Layton then sits up on a rock in a small adjoining creek and sees another deadly Komodo dragon lizard walking toward him. "Not today buddy, you aren't going to eat me!" he mutters to himself. The pilot runs almost a hundred yards to flee the area. Ed then examines the gunshot wound on his chest. Fortunately the bullet just grazed the skin. He looks up into the sun and jungle canopy above him. "God I hope the others had enough time to escape!" The pilot is overcome with relief and dozes off on the well-concealed riverbank, his justly deserved reward.

The Dutchman and the native guide begin their slow return to the compound.

The Diversion

Komorowski and Ford emerge from behind a building and run forward undetected toward the airstrip. They hide in bushes. Standing before them is the runway with the revetments containing several Japanese zero fighter planes. They carefully slide like snakes from the bush into one of the revetments. Ford cautiously slides along the rear empennage of one airplane to avoid being spotted by sentries posted along the runway.

Daryl carefully takes a bayonet off a rifle and looks over the aircraft skin with his hand. George hands him a sharp rock. The sergeant then punches a single hole beneath a wing fuel tank. The coral sand absorbs the fuel as the knife is withdrawn. Komorowski then pulls a pin on a grenade moments later and tosses it in a growing pool of gasoline beneath the plane. The men run back into the bushes toward the dock. George remarks, "Boy, is this gonna be a good explosion, I can hardly wait to see the huge fireball!" Sergeant Ford, however, grabs the sight-seeing jovial crewman and drags him back into the jungle.

Both men run away with breakneck speed. George blurts out, "C'mon Daryl! You take the fun out of everything! Why can't I stay and watch?"

Ford comments, "Sorry buddy, because it is time to go. This place will soon be swarming with troops. Enjoy the sound and shockwave. Hurry, we got to get to that dock!"

The Radio Message

Associated Press reporter Jerry Argendizo carefully navigates several bushes alongside the radio hut as the sounds of radio communications and Morse code fill the air. He is just about ready to send out the most important story of his career. Within seconds, a large explosion is heard as an aircraft is engulfed in flames. Several of the soldiers at the flight line hit the dirt to avoid the flying debris. Even though they are quite a distance apart, Ed Layton and the baron hear the sound as their eyes scan their surroundings, trying to make sense of the event. Colonel Yakashi is interrupted while taking a bath in his small villa. He shouts, "What in the hell is going on?!" to a nearby soldier. "Damn it! Get me my uniform!" The guard quickly gathers the officer's clothing.

In the radio center, all the personnel go to the main door to see what is going on. Jerry stands up and peers inside the radio room to find it vacant. He hesitates. One Japanese soldier runs past and yells to the radiomen, "Sergeant Ito, one of our aircraft has exploded!" The senior radio sergeant replies, "That is horrible news! I will remain at my post. Maybe I will have to send out a message for Colonel Yakashi!" He then pushes his assistant radio operator to join the soldier at the airfield. "Boy, go and help out at the airfield, I can manage." The teenage soldier acknowledges. "Yes Sir!" and joins the other man for a quick sprint to help put out the blaze. The last thing the island needs is to have the smoke from the inferno lead the Allies right to them. Jerry determines that the coast is clear and climbs into the radio room from a window. He studies the equipment carefully. His eyes then find a convenient map with all the longitudes and latitudes his heart would desire. The American seats himself in the chair while Sergeant Ito remains outside in the doorway smoking a cigarette. Argendizo then scribbles down rough coordinates to the baron's island on a slip of paper. He adjusts the Morse code radio equipment and begins to type a message on an open frequency.

Bugs Bunny, 265217. Held captive by baron on island. Northeast of New Britain, Zero degrees South...

Within minutes, Sergeant Ito walks back into the radio room and finds it occupied by an uninvited guest. The startled news reporter suddenly jumps from his chair and quickly draws his knife, which he recovered from one of the soldiers. He handles it as though he was back on the rough streets of Brooklyn. He twists the knife in his hands with great skill to impress his enemy. Sergeant Ito begins several martial arts moves. The New Yorker's determination is matched by the samurai discipline of Sergeant Ito standing before him without facial expression. The sergeant measures up his adversary. Jerry is now nervous and says, "Take one step forward *Tojo*, and you're chicken chow mein!"

Jerry delivers a few unsuccessful jabs toward the soldier, each attempt easily avoided by the Japanese's catlike reflexes. The sergeant smiles as both men circle the room trying to get into the best attack position. Sweat rolls down both of their faces in this duel to the death. The soldier then delivers a swift kick, toppling Jerry as he loses his knife under the nearby table. The men wrestle on the floor until the reporter eventually strangles the man to death with a radio headset cord. He jumps back into the chair and tries to get his bearings to resend another message to the ears of the Allies, but he is thwarted as two more soldiers, with pistols drawn. The men attack Jerry and beat him to a pulp in the room. The unlucky American will now have an appointment with Colonel Yakashi and probably a firing squad for the murder of the head radio specialist.

The Horse Chase

After the explosion at the airfield, Lieutenant Randy Foster runs along a path toward the stables located near the troop camp and field kitchen. He slides under the fence into the corral. The horses are startled, but he calmly comforts them with skills from his ranch in Texas. He fancies a beautiful white stallion, Colonel Yakashi's mount. He gently strokes the horse, "Hey, I have seen you before. You look absolutely beautiful. I bet you're the colonel's prize possession! Steady boy!" Tex then climbs aboard the stallion. He gets a feel for the animal and calms the horse with kind words, "I'm sure you won't mind if I take you out for a little joy ride, eh? Show me how good you are. Steady! I bet you want out of here just like I do. Maybe you can show me the way to the dock area." He strokes the animal's mane. The Texan then commences a full gallop toward the bamboo fence. A Japanese soldier takes notice of the informal rodeo and fires off several unsuccessful shots with his rifle into the air, shouting, "Stop! Stop! Or the colonel will kill you for stealing his horse!" The American pilot ignores the shouts, accelerates the stallion to full gallop, and successfully clears the corral fence.

Foster gallops down a main road toward the Japanese camp. Behind him, another soldier sounds alarm and is picked up by a passing truck. They begin their pursuit of the copilot. The colonel and his men congregate outside his bungalow. Yakashi's eyes are then suddenly drawn to the roadway as an unidentified horseman makes his approach. The colonel walks several feet towards the porch railing to get a closer look at the rider and calmly takes a sip from his mess cup. The sight of Lt. Foster riding his horse outrages him. He slams his drinking cup to the ground and commands his men to begin their pursuit. One Japanese soldier standing near the colonel smiles, points, and in broken English remarks "Ah... cowboy!" as he observes the horse pass by. The colonel then commences a verbal tirade at the soldier as Tex hurtles a single grenade towards him as he rides past. It explodes into a ball of fire, killing two soldiers. Randy's pistol guns down another soldier who impedes the path of his horse.

The rough rider shouts "Yeehaw!" as though he's on another great western roundup and disappears into the jungle. The army truck, still following closely behind, plows right into the brush. Amid a hail of gunfire, the copilot lets his last grenade inconspicuously fall from the horse directly into the path of the vehicle. It explodes, and the truck rolls over in a fireball. The Japanese troops are unsuccessful in their chase and watch as Randy is swallowed up by the jungle. Colonel Yakashi is embarrassed by the loss of his prized horse and vows revenge. One soldier who missed the action comes up to him a bit late and reports to the colonel, "Colonel, Colonel! Your horse has been stolen!"

Yakashi acknowledges, "Yes Soldier! Don't worry. The American can't go far. Remember, we are on an island. My horse can't swim either!"

Message Received Loud and Clear

At the Royal Air Force unit in Port Moresby, the operations room is business as usual as the daily flow of intelligence information is being processed. Major Clark is standing before the large map once again. She carefully evaluates the military situation. Corporal Moneypenny walks up behind her to share the latest haul of aerial reconnaissance photographs. The pictures are in an enclosed, string-wound envelope.

"Major, here are some more photographs taken over Rabaul. Can I see some of the pictures? How can I be expected to learn if you don't let me…?"

Samantha cuts off her sentence in consolation, "Not now corporal, later perhaps. I must pass these on to Lieutenant Loxley for evaluation. She can determine the type of ships sunk, cargos lost and damaged. With her latest optical equipment she could tell if you cut your parents' grass back in Manchester. Nothing escapes her attention." The girl then walks away to her desk slightly frustrated. Moneypenny has such a burning desire to get more deeply involved in espionage. Major Clark gives off a look of genuine sympathy to the girl. Clark then walks past a row of desks to Lieutenant Loxley's workstation.

"Flight Officer Loxley, look what the milkman brought for you this morning." Carol is staring intently through her optical magnifier over a seemingly crucial photograph.

"One moment Major. I think I've got it...Yes, it is all so clear. When our pilots said they scared the pants off the Japanese on the ground below, they're not kidding. Mmm...these low-level camera passes are always so interesting. You can see everything!" Everyone in the immediate vicinity starts to laugh. "Yes Major, what do you have for me?"

Carol's boss sets down another packet of aerial photographs and comments, "The latest prints from some reconnaissance off Rabaul. Taken before the nasty typhoon hit the area." Loxley opens the packet of newly taken photos, thumbs through them, and remarks, "Yes, these are very good photographs. Look here, on this dock area, a harbor area full of troops and lorries." She continues to stare at the photos.

Major Clark then notices General Kingston and the Sergeant Major walking toward them. Clark comments, "Oh, here comes the Sergeant Major again, the one who fancies you."

Loxley is irritated, "Tell him to get stuffed!" Then the major teases the photo recon expert a bit, "With General Kingston!" The lieutenant then quickly organizes her desk and stands up to greet both men.

"Afternoon ladies, I have just received this message, cleared through intelligence in Brisbane. It was provided by an Australian destroyer and a coast watcher. It appears to be some kind of distress message. Let me read it to you all."

"BUGS BUNNY 265217. HELD CAPTIVE BY BARON ON ISLAND NORTHEAST OF NEW BRITAIN ... ZERO DEGREES SOUTH... (UNCLEAR) EAST... GERMANS...STRIKE IMMEDIATELY!"

ARGENDIZO

AP

"What do you make of this?" He hands the dispatch to reconnaissance expert Loxley while Sergeant Major Walter Baldwin then sits down on a nearby chair to witness the unfolding verbal duel before him. He pivots his head between the two during the debate. The lieutenant carefully examines the document, shakes her head with disappointment, and replies "Well... I shouldn't believe it. It's probably just another decoy... a trap. *Bugs Bunny...*

Now things are becoming quite silly, don't you agree? Nonsense." She then hands the paper to Major Clark standing beside her and remarks to the general, "Remember what happened two months ago? Sir. The Japanese, crafty buggers as they were, sent out a false message and our rescue party flew right into an ambush. A massacre! How soon we forget." General Kingston staunchly disagrees and follows his gut instinct. He shakes his head back and forth indicating his displeasure.

"*Bugs Bunny 265217*" Hmmm..." the general mutters to himself. "It could be the name and tail number off a Yank aircraft." Baldwin comments.

Carol quickly interrupts, "Yes Sergeant Major, a brilliant deduction. The Japanese probably got the number off a hunk of fuselage for all we know." Baldwin, with a crush on the officer, then agrees with the sexy woman and then turns to the general to hear his explanation with a look of skepticism. General Kingston now recognizes that he has the floor in the discussion.

"I had toured some Eighth Air Force bases in England last year when these Americans arrived. They can have a wild imagination when it comes to painting their planes... must be the beer."

General Kingston continually follows his instincts and refuses to let the matter rest. "This abbreviation, A.P., sounds like the Associated Press. The bloke may be a reporter... An American no doubt about it."

Loxley smiles and chuckles. "From a dog tag picked from the body of a dead airman." Kingston then continues. "This person... dead or alive, also mentioned something about Germans, and this whets my curiosity. I'm sure Admiral Mountbatten has seen this intercept. I wonder what else Ultra at Bletchley has found out." The general walks over to the map on the wall and explains, "We know that the Germans have had a U-boat base at Penang, East Indies, for some time, further west. According to our coast watchers and destroyer, the transmission seemed to be emanating from this area right here, around Nauru Island." He points to a spot on the map. Loxley is visibly uncomfortable as the officer's finger crosses over a location near the baron's island.

"General, maybe the Jerries have setup another base?" snaps Sergeant Major Baldwin. (Jerries was a World War I British slang term for Germans).

Clark agrees and comments, "Plausible."

The general continued, "I am very surprised that Bletchley hasn't found anything mentioned in this area from the decryption of the German and Japanese naval codes. We've been reading them since the war started... I don't like this gap in our information. It's like looking out a window covered in frost. Can't see a bloody thing. Someone else may have picked up the same transmission. In the meantime, I suggest that we begin a basic aerial search pattern here off Nauru Island until we hear from our other radio surveillance teams once again. Maybe this Argendizo will send another message. Whoever this baron is, he's obviously well hidden." The officer turns to Samantha. "Major Clark."

She replies immediately, "Sir."

Kingston continues. "I would like for you to notify one of our PBY Catalina's to patrol that area and see if they can spot something. Maybe Lieutenant Loxley can find us another sub base." He again turns to the large map, "Probe as far north as the Kapingamarangi Atoll. This ocean is quite wide, and we're going to need all the luck in the world to find the aircrew, and baron, if they even exist." Kingston heads for the door and summons Baldwin commenting, "Sergeant Major Baldwin, I'd like to see you in my office." The door to the command center closes behind them.

Upon reaching the general's office they are seated for a brief discussion concerning their photo interpreter. "Sergeant Baldwin, I know that you are still getting settled in since you arrived two weeks ago. It has come to my attention that you have been chasing Lieutenant Loxley around this base, making somewhat unprofessional advances towards her. This behavior must cease at once. We desperately need for her to be free from distraction, since we're at a critical moment in the war with this whole Rabaul-Bougainville campaign. We need her eye in the sky now more than ever before." The Sergeant Major nods his head in acknowledgement as the lecture continues. "Carol has fought long and hard to get this assignment in the Far East. Whether you know it or not, she was instrumental in providing good aerial interpretation for the Bruneval raid off the coast of France last year when we nabbed a German radar set right from under their noses. I'd consider her to be Sidney Cotton's daughter for all the brilliant work she's done so far." (Referring to the preeminent British aerial photography spy).

"Please leave her alone. Besides, she's still mourning over the loss of her husband." Baldwin looks on with intense speculation. "Wounds take time to heal, and you better respect that…This is your first and last warning."

The sergeant major then nervously remarks, 'Sir, begging your pardon, I didn't know…I was unaware." He bluffs the officer.

The general then comments with growing irritation, "You young lads have it too good. When I was your age, serving as a forward observer for the Royal Field Artillery in the trenches of Neuve Chapelle, I was more concerned if Fritz was going to drop another Whizz Bang on the 'ole Napper. (Whizz Bang was a nickname for a World War I German small artillery shell that whizzes through the air and explodes).

Many of the chaps in my group never made it back to Blighty, just buried in some rat-infested hole. Nonetheless, we cannot have you chasing her around." The sergeant major understands, salutes the general, and leaves his office.

The Spy in Action

Major Clark is busy in her office, assembling the intelligence papers and measuring the distances on the map in reference to the supposed location of the mystery transmission. She plots all of the coordinates carefully and writes them in her logbook. Loxley resumes her work studying aerial reconnaissance photographs with her magnifier. From her desk, Carol's eyes watch her commander's every move from the open office door intently. The security of Vandermeer's entire drug smuggling operation and secret German project could now be in jeopardy. The flow of solid cash into her Swiss bank account may end abruptly. The lieutenant quietly taps her pencil on her desk and then contemplates a new course of action. Within seconds the devilish woman makes her decision. She removes her glasses and leaves the operations room.

The attractive woman walks out of the heavily sandbagged operations building and heads to see Major Simon Evans, the doctor on station. She enters his office, and the man is seated at his desk.

"Ah Lieutenant, so nice to see you this afternoon. What's troubling you?" The good-hearted doctor extends his hand for a pleasant handshake.

"Well Major Evans, since the whole operation against Rabaul began this month, I can't for the life of me get any sleep at night. I know that we are all in this for God, King, and Country, but it's starting to wear me out." Loxley continues. "I toss and turn at night thinking of our brave lads out there. I'm just very tense and wondering if you have something for me."

"Well" the doctor replies, "I might just have something ...one moment..." The doctor opens up his medicine cabinet. "These are sleeping tablets. They are a bit strong and will make you sleep pleasantly, I can assure you. Take only one with a glass of water before going to bed. Not during duty hours. We need you to stay sharp; after all, you're our top girl. The war is far from over, you know. How you can study those recon pictures with the magnifier for hours just amazes me." A nice smile appears on Carol's face. "Thank you so very much." She pats the doctor on the shoulder and exits the room, leaving a smiling doctor behind. He shakes his head, whistles, and says to himself, "What a woman!"

The lieutenant eventually returns to the operations building and her desk. Her devious eyes again return to scan Major Clark's office and glances at the nearby coffeemaker. The spy springs into action as she walks to the commander's office. She peeps into the door. "Would you like a cup of tea? It looks like it's going to be a long afternoon," Loxley asks.

Major Clark accepts with pleasure. "Absolutely, I need it to help me during my work on this triangulation of radio traffic, with that A.P. press leak. It is now Carol's golden opportunity to derail the next reconnaissance sweep for the baron's island before it can get off the ground.

The traitorous woman goes into an adjoining room to prepare the special drink. After dropping two tablets into the tea destined for her colleague, Loxley's hands close the top of the medicine bottle. Suddenly Baldwin enters the room, startling the young woman. She quickly conceals the bottle in her hands. "Walter! You just about scared the knickers off me!"

He answers with a chuckle, "Just my intention!"

Carol continued, "I thought that you were off for the rest of the day?"

"Well, I was, but now when I see you here, I may have to hang around a bit!" remarks Walter with his eyes gleaming for her. Carol's hands continue to conceal the bottle of pills, and she realizes she has to get back to Samantha quickly to prevent her from contacting an aerial reconnaissance group. The clock is ticking, and time is running out. She has to get rid of Baldwin quickly. The Raven (the code name of baron's agent) realizes that a German U-boat is due to surface momentarily near the island to unload crucial equipment onto what is apparently an innocent-looking civilian yacht. The last thing she needs is for the submarine to surface right under the shadow of an Allied aircraft.

"Well Walter, let me get back to my desk. No time to chit chat at the moment. I'm sure that we could get together later this afternoon at the beach. How about three o'clock?" Walter cautiously agrees and leaves the room. She takes the cup and saucer, carefully mixing it, and returns to the Major's room.

"Sounds to me like Walter is at it again," remarks Samantha.

Loxley replies, "He sure is...that Scouse! Here you are."

The officer accepts the cup and inconspicuously wipes crumbs from her mouth of the pastry she had just eaten before accepting the tea. Carol does not immediately take notice. Within several minutes, the soothing cup of tea rests in the officer's stomach. Loxley stares at the clock on the wall, then she eyes the empty plate with crumbs and fork and sees the major don her headset in preparation to radio an Australian long range patrol group. Samantha organizes her papers, map, and clear plastic template with the flight coordinates. The major switches the dials on the radio set. Carol starts to sweat for the first time, a drop gently rolling down the side of her forehead. She again nervously stares at the clock and at the plate. The lieutenant has to stall the officer since the pills won't take effect for the next minute. The clock continues its march towards two o'clock in the afternoon.

Carol begins to carry a slight smile as she notices the officer shake her head and yawn a bit. However, it doesn't seem to stop the determination of the woman from London in following through on her task of notifying the Aussies. Loxley notices that she is ready to deliver the message and suddenly interjects, "Major...are you sure that the Number 4 Recon group is in the best position to send up a patrol into the area? Maybe they were taken out by the typhoon. Haven't you heard, Admiral Spruance's fleet is still a shambles from it. I doubt if many of our Catalinas are still afloat in the area. What are you thinking?"

Lieutenant Loxley walks over to the map and uses her pencil to prove her point. Major Clark remarks, "I heard that an Aussie flying boat, inbound from the island of Truk could carry out a more effective sweep." The officer looks at Carol from the radio looking very groggy. The woman begins to get sleepier in her chair and yawns. While Carol attempts to deliver yet another monologue, the telephone on her desk rings, and she must answer it. She hesitates as the phone continues to ring. "Your phone is ringing my dear." Her boss replies. Samantha then pivots her chair around to key up the microphone to deliver a very tired message to the Australians. Carol walks out of the office and back to her desk telephone with great frustration.

Loxley then is subjected to a rather lengthy telephone call from another officer who requires several key aerial photographs. Her eyes remain glued on Major Clark, but the telephone cord helplessly restrains her. Samantha has notified the Australian patrol group. Carol is very upset as Clark now dozes off into a deep sleep. It is too late. After finishing the call, Lieutenant Loxley angrily walks over to Samantha's office and quietly closes the door behind her. Enraged, she examines the snoozing officer sprawled out on the desktop. Carol then walks over to the radio set and furiously rips the headset cord from the radio jack, muttering, "Bloody hell!" She then paces the room and ponders the next course of action. The woman leaves the operations room for the communications-code room on base to prepare another secret message to Baron Carl Vandermeer, code named, Wolf.

Interception

The Dutchman sits at his desk in his private bungalow, fuming mad about a failed hunt and his escaped prisoners. Colonel Yakashi is present with all three guards that were overpowered by the Americans. He is beside himself and vents his anger. "Colonel, how was this breakout possible? I mean, your men, like those of the *Waffen S.S.* and Indian Legion, were chosen for their expertise! Most minute attention to detail! Cool nerves under pressure! They should have been able to sniff the scent of trouble, and then the prisoners still get away."

The colonel tries to save face, "Well Carl, think of it this way. You have three targets alive in the jungle, just waiting for you to hunt them. Just like you did with the Royal Air Force crew on board that C-47 transport we shot down."

Carl vows revenge while clutching his rifle and angrily reloading it. "Yes, you are right old Chap." He then looks down at his rifle and remarks. "Well... I guess you and I will be working overtime in the next forty-eight hours! Have them get our horses ready." The baron then realizes that one airman is missing. "Ah, Colonel, three men escaped. I thought there was another man?" Colonel Yakashi then quickly clarifies the situation. "Oh yes, we do have another American, the reporter from New York. We have him in the sweat box, solitary confinement." The Dutchman is then smiling with delight,

"Well, that's excellent news! We can use that reporter as bait because I am sure that the rest of the air crew would no doubt.... attempt to rescue him... Good show, we will hold him as bait, a bloody hostage!" The man laughs with delight.

Within seconds, Captain Bhavnani arrives with a message from the radio shack. "I am very sorry for the interruption. You have an important message from Port Moresby." He hands the small paper to Vandermeer. It is an urgent dispatch from Lieutenant Loxley. It reads:

WOLF.

ONE ENEMY AIRCRAFT WILL SWEEP OVER AREA OF U-BOAT RENDEZVOUS. BEARING 120 DE-GREES EAST. ESTIMATED TIME OF INTERCEP-TION AFTER 230 PM TODAY. CANNOT DIVERT.

RAVEN

Carl immediately springs from his desk in distress and shouts to the Indian, "Get me Admiral Brand right away!" The officer turns around and quickly leaves the building. The baron now reads the message to those in the room: "A enemy plane will sweep over area of U-boat rendezvous ... cannot divert!" The Japanese colonel and his men are startled by the dispatch.

Colonel Yakashi replies, "Now this is not what we had anticipated; however, it is only a matter of time before this island would be discovered. I guess today is going to be our unlucky day. We have to tell the U-boat commander to offload another time."

The German naval officer eventually arrives and confronts the baron, who is nervously pacing before him. "You have an urgent message for us *Herr Vandermeer?*" snaps Admiral Brand. The Dutchman replies, "Admiral, I have just received a message from my agent inside the R.A.F. that an enemy aircraft will fly over our area, right when your U-boat is going to offload your critical radio equipment."

The German officer thinks it over. "If they spot our submarine, this whole operation would be terminated immediately, and then I would return to Germany to be hung from a tree in the Berlin Zoo, by *'Der Fuhrer'* "

The men pause and think about possible methods to evade detection. Carl suddenly snaps his finger and declares, "Colonel Yakashi, Admiral Brand! Why not get your fighters up right away to cover the U-280 arrival? An enemy scout plane is sure to be there at 2:30 PM. We have more than enough firepower to clear the sky. Apparently my agent couldn't stop the over flight. Colonel, have the *Luftwaffe* (Air Force) pilot accompany your men in his Messerschmitt. They must take the patrol plane out on the first pass! There must be no message of a submarine." The colonel and admiral agree on the simple solution and both men run out of the building towards the airfield.

At the airstrip, both Japanese carrier pilots and their German comrade in arms are sitting and having a light snack with a cup of tea outside their readiness tent. One of the wrecked Zero fighter planes is being towed off into the jungle, with a new plane being placed into its spot in the heavily sandbagged revetment. One Japanese pilot gives the German *Luftwaffe* pilot a Samurai headband to try on. The pilots see the top brass approaching and stand up from their chairs to receive an important message.

The admiral addresses the pilots, "Men, within the next thirty minutes, our U-boat, the U-280 will be surfacing off the island to deliver some radar-radio equipment. We have received word that a possible enemy plane will be in the area." The German pilot, Heinz Reinmann, who has been languishing in extreme boredom for several months after being assigned to guard the ultra-top-secret radio project, is absolutely thrilled" *"Endlich ein Angriff!"* (Finally an interception!) He could play cards with his *S.S.* comrades only so long to break the inactivity. The naval officer continues. "It is extremely important that you surprise the enemy and bring it down without any radio message being transmitted. Understood! If the Allies discover anything about the secrets of our project *'Merkur'*, *Der Fuhrer* and Admiral Doenitz will be most displeased." One Japanese pilot answers, "Rest assured Sir, we will bring the aircraft down, many miles from here."

The pilots grab their flight gear and race for their aircraft. The men are helped aboard the two Japanese fighters, while the camouflage tarp is removed from a German Messerschmitt 109G fighter. Reinmann's Me 109G is out of the ordinary when it comes to its unique camouflage paint scheme. The wings are painted with the darkened silhouette of a British Spitfire and side fuselage camouflage is that reminiscent of the Battleship Bismarck, with white and black lines to distort the visual plane of the fighter's actual length. All national insignia has been removed from the German fighter aircraft as an added precaution.

Vandermeer's eyes are then glued to the clock on the wall in his private study. Hanging next to the headhunter facemask, it shows 2:00 PM in the afternoon. The second hand gently moves along the face. Will the pilots be able to shield the U-boat operation from discovery? The timing is crucial. He nervously paces in his office and briefly glances at the old bottle from the World War One German merchant raider. The sounds of the aircraft engines springing to life add a brief momentary smile to the Dutchman's face. The survivors of the *Bugs Bunny* also scan their eyes in the direction of the aircraft noise. The men loading the opium laden oil drums and dockyard guards are also distracted as well. They stop working and walk outside their processing center to get a glimpse of the sleek fighter aircraft.

The planes stand ready at idle, warmed up for the interception. Admiral Brand gives Reinmann the thumbs up and shouts good luck, *"Viel Glück!"* The ground crew and soldiers then stand at attention and salute the men in their flying machines in an impressive show of Axis camaraderie. The *Waffen S.S.*, Japanese, and Indian Legion members salute the brave airmen when the canopies slam shut, as each aircraft taxis onto the runway. Within a minute, two Zeros and one rogue Me109G are airborne. The aircraft race over the island for the target area at full throttle. All of the island's inhabitants notice the impressive flyby.

The admiral and Colonel Yakashi return to the pilot readiness tent. They are joined by their Axis colleagues. Admiral Brand tells the Japanese officer, "It's five after two...I hope your men reach the area in time."

The colonel replies, "These carrier pilots were handpicked by Admiral Koga himself to shield this operation and will not fail. The reputation of the German pilot, of course, speaks for itself."

The Axis formation skims the waves of the beautiful blue Pacific Ocean, racing away from the island. After a safe distance, they climb for altitude. The German pilot stares at his watch, which reads 2:15 PM. Interception should take place in several minutes. The men scan the white puffy clouds for any sign of the Allied plane. They do spot the motor launch, standing at its pre-arranged location, awaiting the arrival of the submarine from Penang. No visual contact yet, even thirty minutes later. The men wonder if the Allied agent has made an error in judgment. The Axis scan the skies like hawks, waiting to catch a glimpse of their yet elusive prey.

At roughly 10,000 feet altitude, a single Royal Australian Air Force Catalina, flown by Pilot Officer Bob Rafferty and his crew, are on the homeward leg of a night mission gone awry. The Australians, serving with the Number 11 Squadron, has been delayed in their return from a nocturnal raid on Truk Harbor with engine trouble. They have been suddenly tasked with finding the lost Americans on their return trip to base. The black painted night raider sticks out in the clear blue sky like a beacon for all to see. The aircraft is painted with letters, "RK-O," synonymous with RKO Pictures in Hollywood, California.

The pilot of the lumbering aircraft, Captain Rafferty, has a word with his copilot. "Hey Willis, how much longer before we turn to port and steer 250 degrees, Mate? Who knows how long the makeshift repair on engine two will carry us. Oh we were so lucky to have had all the tools!" The lieutenant checks his watch and then glances at the radio direction compass and map before him. "We will not make our turn for another 10 minutes Sir, I will advise."

The pilot stares at his copilot with a look of frustration, and answers, "Copy."

"Lieutenant, we haven't spotted as much as a Sampan in the last two hours. As you know, we normally fly at night. Our "Cat" sticks out like a sore thumb in the daylight. HQ must be onto something really big."

Lieutenant Willis responds, "Well, at least we got the mines laid. Pity we had to abort our return last night. Didn't use much ammunition on that one, so if any enemy aircraft do come to pick a fight, I think our girl here will see us through. She always has. Remember, our ship has three kills so far. Maybe we can bag a few more." The copilot then takes a drink of his Coke. "What really bugs me is why in the hell do we have to try and find the missing Yank B-25, leave it to the R.A.F. leave us the bloody pommies alone." (Pommies is a slang Australian term for "Prisoners of His Majesty" in early Australian penal colonies of England's royal crown).

In the skies above, one of the Japanese pilots spot the enemy floatplane. Lieutenant Osato radios his team. "Comrades, one heavy, approaching from the left, at about two o'clock. See him?" The silhouette of the black Australian aircraft is seen in the clouds.

Reinmann acknowledges. "I see him Takeo, men, descend to 10,000, and I'll make one head on pass. You jump on him from above and behind. This should be easy." He continues in German, thrilled about finally seeing action against an enemy aircraft after so many months of boredom: *"Endlich einen Angriff auf ein feindliches Flugzeug!"* He instinctively grabs the throttle control and boosts to full power. The noise of his Daimler Benz engine roars as he begins a dive on the flying boat.

The silence aboard the Australian plane is shattered by a rear crewman peering out of a large blister side observation window. "Captain! I just spotted two Japanese Zeros off to our left! They are coming down at us now!" All the crewmen frantically look out for more enemy aircraft out their windows. The copilot then remarks. "There aren't any Japanese aircraft carriers or islands out here! We are too far away from Rabaul. This doesn't make any sense!"

Rafferty gets on the interphone and notifies the crew. "All right men, here we go, undertaking evasive action! Brace yourselves." Within seconds a lone aircraft is framed in the cockpit window.

Lieutenant Willis shouts alarm. "Sir, one lone aircraft approaching from head-on! We've got to move now!" The pilot acknowledges and takes the control column and begins to manhandle the plane into a tight turn.

The nose-mounted 50-caliber machine guns on the aircraft greet the German pilot. At that instant, Heinz Reinmann peers into his Revi gunsight and fires his weapons. *"Jetzt habe ich dich, Schwarze Katze!"*("Now I've got you, Black Cat!"). His guns belch fire and score several hits on the front of the Australian flying boat. The Messerschmitt, however, takes a pasting with holes opening up on the right wing. The pilot and copilot of the robust PBY are extremely experienced in aerial maneuvers and will not take this interception lightly.

In the rear section of the PBY Catalina, the waist guns spring to life. "Tally Ho! Bandits I'll get them! Bastards!" is shouted over the interphone system. The flying boat's 50-caliber waist guns hurl tracer bullets at the two Japanese fighters as the rogue Messerschmitt flies past. The Japanese pilots manage a few hits on the aircraft after plunging downward. Several more passes are made on the rugged Catalina. One crewman alerts the pilot to the rogue fighter plane. "Sir! I just saw that first plane as it raced passed us yet again. It was a strange craft, never saw anything like it. It was not a Jap Tony fighter, since it didn't have the belly air scoop on it and it has the wings of a Spitfire. I will try and get another close look at it on the next pass." Captain Rafferty concurs, "We saw it for a brief second as well. It is hard to make out the contours of the plane. Collins! Get a message out to our base. We are under heavy attack, give them our position!" The radioman begins his Morse code message and comments, "The blokes don't call us RKO radio for nothing, and now for my next broadcast!"

The waist gunner yells out once again, "Sir, Two Japanese approaching again, six o'clock. Get us outta here!"

The lumbering plane then begins evasive action and climbs into a thick cloudbank. The enemy planes briefly lose their prey. The enemy fighters remain in their distinctive "V" formation and circle the clouds. *"Wo ist der Kerl?"* ("Where is the guy?") the German pilot curses from his cockpit. In a break in the clouds the R.A.A.F. aft observer spots the rogue fighter and then shouts, "Mates, you aren't going to believe this. I just saw a Messerschmitt Me 109! What in the...? A Messerschmitt out here, unbelievable! Not even a swastika on her tail or markings on the wings. I sure as the hell know a 'Schmitt when I see one! What in the world is going on here?" Rafferty shouts to his radio operator, "Collins, add the Messerschmitt to your report!" The Catalina breaks out of the clouds and is engaged once again by enemy fighters. The 50-caliber guns on the flying boat nose turret then score a lucky hit on the Me-109 engine cowling during another head on pass. A cloud of vapor trails from the stricken fighter as the aircraft takes a hit in the coolant system. The *Luftwaffe* pilot observes the damage and curses, *"Ach du Scheisse!"* (Oh Shit!) and is forced to bail out moments later as the engine bursts into flames. The men aboard the "Cat" yell out with cheer as the German fighter streaks off trailing smoke.

The Japanese pilots are enraged at the loss of their comrade and press home their attack on the lone target. The PBY is also starting to show smoke trailing off one engine. Captain Rafferty tells his copilot, "Feather number one! We got a fire!"

A crewman suddenly shouts, "Captain! Two bandits coming back again, at six, and closing!" The aircraft's aft 50-caliber guns once again claw out at the enemy pursuit planes. The pilot grabs the control yoke and commences another tight turn. Multiple bullet strikes are heard striking the aircraft. Rafferty yells out, "Collins! How is your broadcast to HQ? Has it been acknowlededged? I don't know how much longer..."

The radioman cues up his microphone with great haste to reply, "I have sent it out, no acknowl..." Within an instant, the Australian Catalina explodes into a ball of flame. The crew is killed instantly. The wreckage spirals downward into the Pacific Ocean.

Carl, Colonel Yakashi, and Admiral sit in the baron's office awaiting news of the ensuing air battle. A Japanese corporal then bursts into the room and happily declares, "The enemy patrol plane has been shot down and our planes are returning to base!" There are shouts of joy in the room and *"Banzai!"* The Admiral and Japanese Colonel happily share a strong handshake as the Admiral exclaims, "Now to tell our U-boat that it can surface. All is clear!" One *Waffen S.S.* soldier replies, "That was a close one, now it's time to celebrate!"

Major Bhanvani looks at the men and offers his two cents. "When the radio transmitter is off loaded at the dock, then we can celebrate!" The men in the room share a laugh among themselves. The Japanese corporal who brought in the message now reads the next portion of the radio message. He quickly loses his smile. "Gentlemen, Men… please…shhh…apparently, uh, the Messerchmitt pilot has been shot down." The room is now completely silent, virtually frozen in time. The Dutchman reaches for the old bottle from the *S.M.S. Wolf* and cradles it in his hands, assuring himself that his island is safe once again.

"Carol, I think we made it."

Within the span of one half hour, two Zero fighter planes land on the island airstrip. The colonel arrives at the edge of the airfield amid the shouts of *Banzai* by the Japanese soldiers cheering on their victorious pilots. The engines sputter to a halt as their canopies slide back. Colonel Yakashi, with Admiral Brand standing beside him, asks a pilot of the fate of the German. "He was shot down and probably drowned. I lost sight of the Messerschmitt in the clouds. No parachute seen," he replies. The German pilot is presumed dead, and the German contingent leaves the airfield in deep sorrow. Reinmann was a top fighter ace, avid card player, and socialite. His presence would be missed. Admiral Brand walks away into the jungle with tears in his eyes. The colonel then returns to the compound. Out in the high seas, roughly twenty miles from the island, the German U-boat from Penang has surfaced, with the motor launch pulling up alongside, awaiting the cargo transfer. *"Vorsicht!* Careful!" is shouted among the recovery crew. The German engineering team will finally get their hands on the radio transmitter for Project *Merkur* after it is offloaded in the next hour.

The secret of the Baron's Island was saved…or so it seemed.

The Escape to Sea

Sergeants Komorowski and Ford brave their way through the dense jungle toward the dock area. The heads of the men emerge from the bushes to survey the area. To their far right are several motorboats and to their left sits the luxury yacht carefully concealed under camouflage netting. *Waffen S.S.* and Indian Legion soldiers congregate on the dock and carry on a discussion in the presence of a Japanese guard. Another Japanese sentry is posted several yards away at the end of the dock.

George is frustrated and whispers his concern. "We are never going to get out of here... Look at all these guys! Where are Ed, Randy, and Jerry? I don't see them. I wonder if they all got caught and executed." The Cherokee is quiet, accessing his options, and tries to calm his excited colleague. "Shh... This doesn't look good. I think we're on our own," he mutters. The men stay hidden for nearly forty-five minutes with no sign of the others. A single Japanese sentry walks by them with a gun slung over his shoulder. He paces back and forth. Sergeants Komorowski and Ford gently walk along the bushes following the soldier as he walks toward the motor launch area. The distance to the boat launch is roughly seventy-five yards.

The Japanese soldier takes a break on the dock and feels that there is something inside his boot. The other guards observe the soldier from a distance as he sits down. Their view is now partially obscured by foliage. In the wake of the *Luftwaffe* pilot's death, the soldiers lighten things up by joking among themselves about the size and chubby appearance of the Japanese soldier standing before them. One soldier comments, , "*Schau Dir seinen fetten Bauch mal an, er sieht so aus wie ein Wildschwein!*" ("Look at his big gut, he looks like a big wild pig!"). The men laugh to the irritation of the guard, who wonders what is so damn funny.

The Polish boy from the south side of Chicago lies down low as Daryl Ford quietly slithers forward like a snake to the Japanese soldier removing his boot. With the blood of his Native American ancestors, the Cherokee of the great plains of America pumping through his veins, the Indian reaches striking distance. George holds his breath and covers his eyes with fright.

Daryl grabs the soldier by the neck and quickly pulls him into the bushes. The sergeant chokes the soldier to death and begins to strip off his clothes. A moment later, Daryl quickly assumes the position of the soldier wearing the Japanese uniform. He grabs the boots and attempts to fit them to his feet. No good, they're too small. Daryl would have to go barefoot. He then paces slowly up and down the dock with a gun in his hands and pauses momentarily to watch the other soldiers from a distance. George scans the jungle once again to try to catch a hopeful glimpse of his comrades. Nothing is seen or heard from their fellow crewmen. He mutters to himself, "C'mon guys, hurry up, damn it! We can't hold this dock area for long!" The motor launch carrying the communications equipment is now seen on the horizon. The Axis soldiers are distracted and try to catch a glimpse of the incoming vessel. They converse with each other.

On the concealed luxury yacht, one soldier steps down onto the dock with a big bottle of Schnapps. The *S.S.* man tells the others that they should each have a shot of liquor to celebrate the transmitter recovery effort. The men take off their military metal drinking cups and await their drink. A discussion with the men begins, and it is agreed to share one glass with the distant Japanese soldier, unknowingly played by Sergeant Ford. Two *S.S.* men, bottle in hand, begin their walk to the motor launch area to offer the drink. Daryl sees the men coming toward him, but he keeps his composure. He then turns his back to pace away towards his comrade. Komorowski spots the enemy troops as well. "Daryl, there are two guys coming! What in the hell are we gonna do?!" Sergeant Ford replies in a whisper, "George, will you shut up? I will take them out, and then we'll jump into the first boat!" It is now do or die, to leave the baron's island with or without their comrades. He tells Komorowski, "I will signal you to run out, jump into a boat, untie the rope, and start the motor running. Capisce!"

Ford gently removes a pistol from the holster and holds it at his waist. Within moments, the *S.S.* men approach to offer the glass of Schnapps. "*Schnapps Mein Herr?*" (Would you like Schnapps, Sir?). One takes note of the soldier's missing combat boots.

With his back to the Germans, Ford yells out, "Now!" The soldiers are startled as the sergeant pivots and fires the handgun. The two German soldiers crumble under the hail of bullets to the dock planking. Komorowski then darts from the bushes, runs briefly along the dock, and jumps into a boat. He quickly casts off the lines and starts the engine. Ford gathers the MP-40 weapons, and extra magazines from the dead soldiers, the liquor bottle, and grenades, and jumps into the boat. The other enemy soldiers see the killing and race down the dock to engage the Americans.

After the lines are removed, the throttle is opened wide as the boat swings left parallel to the launch area heading for the exit of the small cove. Axis soldiers close in on them with their machine guns drawn. Daryl fires at them as their pursuers dive for cover in the nearby bushes. They would have to fight their way past other armed men standing along the dock waiting for the boat with the radio equipment to arrive.

As the escaping boat approaches the dock exit, the remaining *S.S.* men open fire at it with their *Schmeisser* machine guns. Komorowski steers the boat clear as they take a few bullet holes in the side. George then quickly crouches down as Ford empties several bursts towards the enemy, pinning them down. Ford now lies down in the boat to avoid gunfire and fires a couple bursts from the stern. He removes a magazine and inserts a fresh one into the weapon. The water craft develops remarkable speed as it heads for the open sea. The Japanese get on their radio and alert Colonel Yakashi.

In the baron's office, the Japanese corporal returns to the doorway yet again to deliver an ominous message. "Colonel Yakashi Sir! Colonel Yakashi! Two Americans have escaped in a boat...from our dock!" Both Carl and the colonel are startled and then look at each other. Yakashi utters, "Only one way to stop them!" The baron nods his head in agreement.

Ford and Komorowski are seemingly happy and free as they speed out across the vast expanse of the Pacific. They tried to hold out as long as possible for their lost comrades, but to no avail. They resign themselves to a bottle of Schnapps on the boat. Daryl pops open the Schnapps bottle, takes a gulp, and passes it to his faithful comrade. In a comical fashion, they pass the German motor launch carrying the secret equipment and make faces, imitating Adolf Hitler, with shouts of *"Heil Hitler"* arm salutes, and then extending their middle fingers with joy at the Nazis. George even scoffs at the Axis in Polish, telling them to kiss his ass.

The unarmed German crewman aboard the yacht look bewildered. One seaman remarks, *"Was ist denn hier los?"* (What is going on?). Within minutes however, the Americans begin to study the construction of their speedy mount. Ford crawls forward toward the bow and yells out over the engine noise, "Boy! This baby can really move. I wonder what she has under the hood?" He opens up the top cover and is horrified by his find. His eyeballs double in size, and he shouts to Komorowski, "Jesus Christ! ... This thing is loaded to the kilter with explosives! Land Mines!" He collapses onto his knees. The Indian backpedals to the stern, trembling on all fours as if he's seen a ghost. George remarks with a slight chuckle, "Oops! I must have grabbed the wrong one." Their ride continues without interruption, or so it seems.

Within ten minutes, the sound of a piston engine plane is heard in the distance. A Japanese fighter scrambled from the baron's island appears and then begins its first strafing run on the escaping men coming astern.

George grips the wheel firmly in his hand as Ford instructs him to turn left or right in their evasive maneuvers. The Indian stares at the bird of prey and pits his instinct of survival against the skill of the enemy pilot. He reaches for a German machine gun and steadies his footing. The enemy aircraft is almost upon them. "Calculate the lead on this guy!" he mutters to himself as he adjusts the gun barrel, giving the aircraft a bit of lead prior to squeezing the trigger.

The nose of the Zero suddenly pivots downward as the plane enters a shallow dive. The pilot is going to open fire! Daryl frantically empties a few rounds at the fighter as it opens up on them with cannon fire. Sergeant Ford shouts out, "Get ready to turn buddy!" Geysers of water from the cannon shells approach the boat as the aircraft is within a few feet of the daring Americans. "Right!" Ford quickly instructs him. "Turn right!" George then swings the boat to the right and miraculously escapes the first pass.

"Hail Mary full of grace!" Komorowski yells out into the clear blue sky. Ford's gun runs empty. He promptly throws the weapon aside, grabs the next weapon, cocks it, and readies himself for the next pass. He lies down, carefully bracing himself against the boat for a good, clean accurate shot.

The fighter banks into a tight turn and positions for the next pass, which will be from head on. Ford shouts, "Now wait until the rice ball drops the nose of his plane!" George nods in agreement. "He will then open fire!" Daryl and George lock eyes on the fighter in this deadly game of cat and mouse. The Zero drops its nose as geysers of water approach them and Komoroski veers the boat to the left. The plane has missed its target yet again. Both men scream out with joy and curse the enemy pilot.

Within a minute, the fighter once again approaches the speeding boat from astern. "Is that rice ball coming again?" George yells out.

"Yup! He is out for blood George, and I am going to take him out on this next pass, the Jap is flying low enough! One bullet hole into the cylinder head and goodbye Charlie!" The fighter stalks the boat and drops his nose to fire once again. Ford yells out "Right!" once more as he squeezes the trigger.

George manhandles the wheel as he incorrectly assumed they would turn to the left. He corrects his course, but the second of hesitation cost them dearly. Bullets rip into the boat's stern and blow the head clear off George's body. The corpse slumps over the steering wheel and falls to the floor, as the boat's engine is aflame. Daryl is splattered with blood and tissue and shouts into the sky, cursing the pilot over the death of his comrade. He stares at George's lifeless body briefly, remarks, "You will not be forgotten my friend!" and screams with tears in his eyes! The aircraft returns once again to finish the job as the boat has come to a complete stop. Daryl then throws himself overboard amid geysers of bullets. In a matter of seconds the escape craft disintegrates in a fiery explosion. Ford eventually clings to wreckage and rides out the waves in the lonely sea, watching the plane return in the direction of the island.

All is quiet as the debris gently bobbles in the waves. Ford clings to a large section of the boat wreckage and continues crying. The sudden appearance of a shark's dorsal fin changes everything. He climbs aboard the floating remains of the boat's keel and manages to get his body out of the water. The tiger shark circles him out of curiosity for several moments and then swims onward, apparently disinterested. Sergeant Ford breathes a sigh of relief, and suddenly, the boat wreck flips over, capsizing, and tossing the hapless airman back into the water.

The Zero fighter plane wags its wings to signal victory as it flies over the airfield in preparation for landing amid the cheers of the soldiers. *Banzai! Banzai! Banzai!* In Vandermeer's building, a corporal again notifies the staff of the demise of the escaping boat. Colonel Yakashi and the narcotics baron are quite surprised by their persistent luck in keeping their island secret alive. The baron once more stares at the old bottle from the *S.M.S Wolf.* "These were brave men, brave souls…Now they rest quietly beneath the waves in a fitting burial at sea. Quite daring." Carl remarks in an extremely complimentary tone. The colonel then continues, "My men are scouring the island and *will* find the rest of the Americans.

Seaside Rendezvous

The warm late afternoon sun reveals the presence of Lieutenant Carol Loxley quietly strolling along the beach by herself, reminiscing about the hectic events hours earlier. She is dressed in her finest bathing suit and parasol hat, and she sits down on a nearby rock with a sigh and watches the waves at her feet. Walter shadows the woman from a distance and then walks out from behind the bushes and onto the beach. Carol notices him coming and waves in a friendly manner. Upon his arrival he remarks, "How are things this afternoon? You look very tense, more nervous than usual. Anything wrong?" The woman bashfully looks downward and shakes her head in acknowledgement. There is a lot on her mind, with Carl's island on the verge of discovery, and she is still lamenting over her husband's untimely death. He kneels down beside her and wants to get something off his chest. "Carol, I would like to apologize for how I've been acting towards you lately. I know that this is going to be a long war; God knows when it will end. I am sorry about the news of your husband's passing. I uh, didn't know anything about it, honest."

Carol gently pats his hand and tells him that it's okay. She stands up, and they both resume a walk down the surf. "Walter, I do appreciate your sense of humor. It makes it easier on me to get over Paul. My Paul ... God how I miss him. If it weren't for this stupid war, I'd be back home with a family. But that's life for you…full of the unexpected. Why is it that the good people always suffer the most? I'm just fuming over the way he went and how it was handled."

"What happened Carol? Walter gently asks. "If you don't mind my asking." The woman takes in a deep breath and replies, "My husband was a fighter pilot during the Blitz." He was in the Eleventh Group at Kenley, protecting London, and shot down twelve German airplanes. I followed his progress closely, almost religiously. That air war, Walter, was fought over our backyards and doorsteps. Sometimes Paul would fly over our house in the country and wag the wings of his Spitfire for me. We were deeply in love, and after the battle, I wanted to start a family. However, he put it off, citing duty before family. Seemed logical at the time, when Coventry, London started to burn under the Nazi bombs. As for myself, I couldn't just wash dishes and attend tea parties. I wanted to get in on the action. However, when I volunteered to serve in the R.A.F. against the Boche (Wartime Allied nickname for Germans, derived from word cabbage.), he was quite upset—but understood."

Walter sighs "Wow, that took a lot of guts."

The woman continues, "Paul then volunteered to become a test pilot, and one day." She pauses as tears form in her eyes. "He was out testing a new aircraft, the Hawker Typhoon, and on his second flight he vanished like two other pilots several weeks earlier. They searched long and hard until they found the wreckage near Windsor." The sergeant major is stunned into silence.

"The aircraft company launched a preliminary investigation, and they cited "pilot inexperience." That didn't sit well with his comrades at Kenley, and they countered the findings with reports of their own, citing Paul's courage and heroism in combat over London. The chaps at that airfield were a great bunch… had a chance to meet them." Anger then fills the voice of the sorrowful woman. "Then, when the R.A.F. crash team dug deeper, they found that Paul died… he died, of carbon monoxide poisoning! It had seeped into the cockpit from the engine, and he lost consciousness. Upon hearing this I blew up quite naturally and pressed for a lawsuit against the factory, but it didn't get very far.

The government got involved and dashed my efforts. I have been very bitter ever since. My husband's life didn't mean a damn to His Majesty. Good thing I'm over here, boy, would I like to raise the roof in Parliament."

Their walk down the beach continues. The lieutenant asks, "Baldwin, when is the killing going to stop?"

"My thoughts are still with my Paul," She looks up to the sky and whispers, " I miss him so much." The woman then recites a section of a poem written by an R.A.F. pilot who perished during the Battle of Britain.

"Up, up the long, delirious, burning blue, I've topped the wind-swept heights with easy grace, where never the lark, nor even eagle flew. And, while with silent lifting mind (she begins to cry), I've trod the high, untrespassed sanctity of space, put out my hand and touched the face of God."

Baldwin cautiously comforts her with a very respectable hug. Carol and Walter walk onward along the scenic beach as the sun starts to settle near the horizon. Loxley then walks closer, side- by-side with the sergeant major, eventually taking his hand.

Return of the Baron?

Darkness settles on the island as the exhausted captain Layton sits beside a tree and falls asleep in the jungle. After a span of several hours he is jerked awake with fear by the sound of a snorting horse. He is paralyzed with fright, assuming that the baron has finally caught up with him. The tired eyes of the aviator scan the jungle floor, which is enshrouded in a mist, and glimpses the darkened silhouette of a man carrying what appears to be a rifle with his horse. The figure is carefully probing the bushes before him and cautiously studying the ground. The exhausted pilot has had enough of the chase and desires to kill who he thinks is the Dutchman standing before him. He crawls forward through the foliage and eventually football tackles the mysterious man. It is his copilot Randy Foster. There is a sigh of relief between the two as they recognize each other.

"Captain! Ed! It's you! You are still alive! We thought you were dead," blurts out Lieutenant Foster.

"Randy? What in the hell? How'd you get here, and with the colonel's prized horse?" Both men sit down to catch up on the past few missing hours.

"When you were being hunted down like a prairie dog, we broke out of the stockade. We scattered. I think Jerry got to the radio hut and sent out the S.O.S. I tried to get to the dock, but there were too many of the Axis there, so I rode off and hid with this horse, until I bumped into you."

Layton remarks, "I wonder if Daryl and George got away? Headed out to sea? I heard the sound of a Zero."

Foster continues, "While I rode to the dock I hear a lot of gunfire, and I saw the fighter plane just like you heard it. I bet the two did get away, whether or not they survived is anyone's guess."

Layton devises a new course of action. "Park this horse somewhere, and let's get some rest. Tomorrow we have to steal a boat. I want out of this hell just like you."

Randy comments, "It's great to see you again, back from the dead!"

The captain is just as delighted and chuckles, "You're my wingman to the end comrade. We have to watch out for each other. We'll make it, riding on your little bag of luck." The Texan stands up and ties up the horse for the night. The men fall asleep in the jungle under the cloudless sky and bright stars above.

'Merkur' Awakes.

During the night, both Carl and Colonel Yakashi climb into their scout car with two soldiers and speed off into the jungle to witness the first operational test of *Merkur*, the ELF (Extremely Low Frequency) radio transmission station. The German–Japanese research team is assembled and waiting. It will be a festive occasion, with cases of wine, beer and foodstuffs from Germany, delivered from the submarine base at Penang, Dutch East Indies.

The men observe the German transmitter under operation in the darkness with the perimeter closely guarded by a detachment of *Waffen S.S.* It is camouflaged and well-hidden from the prying eyes of Allied aircraft. Outside a concrete bunker, a team of Axis scientists and engineers greet Vandermeer with cordial handshake and Colonel Yakashi with a salute. They thank the Japanese colonel for keeping the American aircraft away. The sound of a diesel generator in a sandbagged dugout echoes throughout the jungle. The men congregate outside.

Admiral Brand begins to brief Carl and the colonel, carefully pointing out the various parts and components. "Gentleman, you have arrived just in time. We will be proceeding with our first test of our *Funkmessgerat* radio transmission station. The transmitter from our U-boat is now in position, as you can see. Our technicians finished the installation this afternoon, and we will be ready to test in several minutes." Then, before the conversation could continue, a technician walks from the bunker and interrupts, advising the group that the unit is ready to broadcast.

"Herr Doktor, das Geraet ist jetzt Einsatzbereit."(The unit is now ready for operation.). The admiral smiles and then ushers the group into the concrete bunker.

"It seems that we are now ready to go, an hour ahead of schedule. Gentlemen, if you please." The naval scientist's lecture continues. "We know that by utilizing long wave technology, in this case directing a sharp beam, you can change the frequency band of the radio spectrum. This allows you to communicate with submarines over great distances with minimal interference of seawater. We have constructed a similar unit in Magdeburg, Germany, called *Goliath. (*An original German Navy *'Goliath'* unit still survives in operating condition in Nizhny Novgorod, Russia. It had been removed from war torn Germany in 1947, and painstakingly rebuilt in 1952. It transmits time signals worldwide for the Russian Navy).

This station, *Merkur,* is half the size of the original unit, with the addition of our latest vacuum tube technology. It has taken us two years to build this device, in cooperation with my colleagues in Japan. *Merkur,* as the technician told us, is alive and well. Observe, gentleman." A Japanese scientist hands Doctor Brand a simple light bulb with a loop of wire and connects them together. He then holds the bulb in the air as it illuminates and remarks, "See, it's a kind of magic. With a frequency band of 15 to 25 KHz." The men laugh. The air is full of electromagnetic activity.

The group smiles as they stand in the operations bunker. The secret antennae complex stands before them in the eerie misty darkness, resembling a large spider in its web. A Japanese scientist then tells Colonel Yakashi, "Colonel, our submarines will also be linked via this transmitter as well. It would allow us to better coordinate our submarine raids on American shipping off their West Coast, like California."

The Japanese officer nods his head in agreement, "Quite an impressive unit. Let's see it do its job. Tokyo will be quite excited."

Before them are several racks of electrical equipment. "Men, this technician has been sending a typed coded message to a U-boat off the coast of Madagascar in the Indian Ocean over the last few minutes. We are waiting for a response. If the link has been established, we have a case of wine and other delicacies from Germany waiting for this momentous occasion. Our timing and positioning have been calculated to precision." The technician on the headset adjusts several knobs and switches. After a few minutes he is startled and again adjusts the equipment. The teletype prints out a message, and the navy technician removes the message with excitement. *"Herr Doktor Brand, Wir haben Kontact!"* (We have made contact!). *"Unglaublich!"* ("unbelievable!"). The soldier almost loses his breath and continues. *" U-500, südöstlich von Madagaskar hat unser Signal empfangen. Kapitän Traut lässt alle grüßen."* (The U-500, lying southeast off Madagascar has received our signal. Commander Traut greets everyone present). Success is at hand. The technician calls Admiral Brand over to him and passes him the document to confirm the findings. The German radio team and engineers let out a rouse of cheers and applause. The German radio technician types out a confirmation signal to commander Traut that his message has been received. He turns to the navy scientist, Admiral Brand, and gives him the thumbs up, *"alles gut!"* Wine bottles and glasses are brought forward and opened. Drinks are distributed to all those present. Admiral Brand gets a few words in to Colonel Yakashi. "Colonel, you have witnessed a remarkable achievement in long distance communications. Nothing will stop us now." After several minutes, the unit generator is powered down. The Germans prepare roast pig, potatoes and bratwurst for the dinner celebration. After the late dinner, the baron and colonel return to the compound for another round of chess.

The Uninvited Guest

Luftwaffe pilot Heinz Reinmann, no stranger to the tropical heat, floats in the Pacific with his life vest. The fortune of the German changes the next morning. At daybreak, a United States Navy submarine on patrol for the missing Australian PBY Catalina accidentally picks up the *Luftwaffe* pilot. While being pulled onto a rubber raft, one of the seamen is shocked and remarks, "Look at that uniform and Iron Cross! It's a kraut pilot...Wait 'till the skipper sees him." The luckless *Hauptmann* with slight burns to his face and hands is transferred to the main deck of the submarine amid the eyes of the confused seamen who offer Heinz a cigarette. Another navy midshipman comments, "What in the blazes is he doing out here? Maybe Naval Intelligence can get something out of him. I don't speak German, do any of you guys?" The men shake their heads signaling they didn't.

One sailor says, "I know we got Herman aboard. His parents were from Germany, maybe he can make this pilot spill the beans why he is out here." The pilot then hands his captors the Walter P-38 pistol from his holster, as the war is over prematurely for the native of Breslau, in Silesia. The pilot then exhibits a look of total loss and despair. He briefly buries his face in his hands and takes another puff of the cigarette.

U.S. Naval Intelligence is alerted to the ship's unique find. Frank Knox, head of the Far East Asian section of U.S. Naval Intelligence, discusses the unusual situation with Admiral Nimitz at Pearl Harbor in Hawaii, to which the gray-haired admiral replies, "A German pilot in the middle of the South Pacific is a very serious matter… a very serious matter. Frank, Washington has already been notified. The president wants a detailed search to be conducted to determine the origin of this pilot."

The frustrated intelligence chief then comments, "Admiral, we know that the British ULTRA reports confirm German submarines operating in the vicinity of Morotai, in the East Indies, carrying strategic materials to Japan. The last thing we need is another German air force springing up in the South Pacific. Your carrier pilots already have their hands full." Admiral Nimitz continues, "Notify your chief of naval intelligence operations in the Solomons. We need more clues as to what the Japanese and the Germans are up to! Let's look at our options." The men stare at the map resting on the desk before them.

The Mystery is Solved

General Kingston storms into the operations room the next morning, waving several reports in his hand. "Listen everyone, gather around! I have in my hand, the missing pieces to the puzzle!" All the personnel in the operations room stop working and surround the officer. Lieutenant Loxley and Major Clark look at each other and then at the general. "What is it?" Carol remarks.

"Remember the transmission we received two days ago regarding *Bugs Bunny*? Well apparently our sources have identified aircraft 265217 as an American B-25 Mitchell bomber attached to the 823rd bomb group piloted by a Captain Edward Layton. Argendizo is an Associated Press correspondent— Jerry Argendizo from New York. The aircraft was posted missing in action in a raid (walks to the large map) on a Japanese troop convoy heading for Bougainville. Several ships on the outer fringes of Admiral Spruance's fifth fleet— coast watchers on New Ireland, our group— and an American radio intercept team on Vella Lavella had also detected the transmission. You see, it happened just like I said it would! Taking all the positions of these ear-witnesses into account (points to the spots on the map), through triangulation, we have determined that the source of the message originated at 0 degrees south and 155 degrees east, quite north of New Britain, and I might add, right on the equator. This B-25 aircrew was way off course... must have been a hellacious storm they flew through. It was a God-given miracle they survived at all. This is where our search will be conducted... right here... 0 degrees south, 155 degrees east... just west of Nauru Island." The people in the room are just amazed by the grand announcement, since they have been following this loose tale over the past few days. Kingston continues. "Now another bit of news. This is interesting. An Australian Catalina, returning from a night raid with engine trouble, has disappeared." Carol shows signs of relief in the statement. "However, my hunch was correct all along. The Germans have something cooking in the area." The officer then continues reading from the radio dispatch on the clip board. "Apparently an American submarine, the Swordfish, searching for the Australians, recovered a, one Hauptmann Heinz Reinmann, a pilot with nearly eighty kills to his credit in North Africa with *JG 53*. According to our sources back in London, his father had served as Naval Attaché in Tokyo for quite a few years before the war. Hmmm. Reinmann has been linked to the elite Brandenburg Division reserved for special operations utilizing foreign languages."

"Looks like the pieces are now all coming together," remarks Major Clark.

The general continues, "The pilot is currently in the hands of G-2 Intelligence but has so far revealed nothing, apparently recuperating from his injuries. Not a helpful chap at the moment. Churchill and Lord Mountbatten have already been notified and urge immediate action.

We will use the information available regarding the radio transmission and hopefully move warships into the area from Admiral Spruance's fleet." Carol is now dead quiet.

Kingston remarks, "Well Carol, what do you think of this information? You look like the cat has got your tongue. Is there anything wrong?"

The woman is extremely nervous, with a completely derailed train of thought. "Oh nothing...nothing at all, intelligence is an amazing field. What can we say." Loxley replies in a shaken manner. She struggles to keep her composure.

The general comments for the last time. "Ladies and gentlemen, I will inform you when more news is available." The room erupts with excitement and mild applause. The fate of the baron's island has finally been sealed, and

Lieutenant Loxley sits back down at her desk. The woman is stone cold, without emotion. The general leaves for his office.

Little Corporal Moneypenny strikes up a conversation with her boss Major Clark and Lieutenant Loxley. "Oh I find this all so very exciting! I wish that I could go out on a search for the Americans. To be there on the ground and dispose of this evil baron—how dare he hold these airmen in a cage! Ooh, it just makes me mad!"

Samantha is just amused by the teenager's comments. "Oh really Moneypenny. I could just see it now, you swooping in behind enemy lines, jumping off a plane, and tearing your knickers on the barbed wire!" The officer and sergeant major shake a laugh. "You won't go far in the intelligence field that way my dear, dramatic as it may sound. Maybe you should stick to the desk work. Don't get me wrong, you are a very sharp girl. King and Country can use you for years to come. Think of it."

Corporal Moneypenny sits for a moment to take in the words of advice from her superior. She then gathers some file folders off a nearby desk and replies, "Yes Ma'am, I think you are right. I *have* been reading a bit too many spy novels lately. It did sound good though, didn't it? Apart from the barbed wire and all, I am just so fascinated by spies and secret agents." The woman stares at Lieutenant Loxley.

The sergeant major then quickly enters the operations room. In his hand is another crucial piece of intelligence information. The major confronts the serious-looking coworker. "Sergeant major, where have you been? You missed the general's latest news brief of sorts."

The man can hardly hold back the excitement and quietly exclaims, "Major Clark, I was at the code room…One of the crew of *Bugs Bunny* has been rescued! His name is technical sergeant Daryl Ford."

Carol Loxley suddenly springs back to life. "Walter, that is an incredible bit of news. Bravo!"

Clark comments, "That is excellent sergeant major. I'd get that communiqué to the general right away. He will be quite thrilled, I am sure of that."

The sergeant smiles, "Oh well, off I go, be back in time for lunch! You know how his monologues go." Baldwin quickly heads to Kingston's office.

"You know, Lieutenant. If this American airman has a thorough debriefing with intelligence, this whole puzzle may be solved within hours. Giving us a clear picture of what this baron and his Axis partners are up to."

Lieutenant Loxley agrees whole heartedly. "Yes, Ma'am. It will speed up the end of the war, and you and I can have a nice drink at Picadilly Square."

Sergeant Major Baldwin stands outside General Kingston's office with slight apprehension. The last time he entered the office, he had received a through tongue lashing for chasing after another coworker, which of course he is. He takes a deep breath and knocks on the door. The general acknowledges, and the door is opened. Baldwin enters. "General Sir! We have just received another coded message from Brisbane. One of *Bugs Bunny*'s crew has been rescued!"

The officer is stunned and collects his thoughts. "Rescued? That's excellent M'lad! Did he shed any light on where he was? Disposition of enemy forces and material?"

Walter stares at the piece of paper in his hand and replies, "Let's see, his name is Technical Sergeant Daryl Ford, and he had been in the water for hours before being rescued by an aircraft, and just barely alive. Claimed to have fought off sharks and is quite dehydrated. The rescue team said he was also wearing the uniform of a Japanese soldier. Now that is bloody well crafty. Snookered the Japs on his escape didn't he? The airman is a truly remarkable man, braving the nasty water and all. The sergeant did mention something about Germans during his bedside debriefing with G-2 Intelligence."

The general tips back in his desk chair and comments, with a confused shake of his head. "Quite bizarre, quite. On one hand we have German aircraft in the South Pacific and nabbing Yanks in enemy uniforms. It is a war of deception Sergeant Major. We are preparing a course of action based on the latest information no doubt about it. The Americans will be rescued within the next few hours. The Navy Department in Washington D.C., Whitehall, Bletchley, are all in an emergency meeting as we speak. I need you back in my office in the next thirty minutes when news of any rescue attack force surfaces. I suggest you take a short break—you are going to need it. The ships and planes are being gathered for action."

The operations breakroom is now quiet for the daily lunch break. In the quiet breakroom, Baldwin calmly takes his fresh cup of coffee and is seated at the table. He reads the latest newspaper and nibbles on his sandwich. Carol Loxley enters the room moments later to get herself a cup of coffee and asks if there have been any interesting developments. "Morning Sergeant Major, what did Kingston make of the last radio intercept you handed him? Any news of a planned rescue mission with Monneypenny leading the charge? An attack? Word has been filtering about our building that something big is brewing."

She looks down at her cup. "More than this coffee I am afraid." The sergeant major playfully ignores her and takes another bite.

Loxley becomes very inquisitive and hates being ignored. "Sergeant Baldwin, when is something going to happen? The curiosity will kill me. The enlisted man then toys with her and acts ignorant.

"I don't know..." as he takes a sip of coffee. "Just a few sketchy details, nothing more." The aerial reconnaissance expert now turns up the charm to get the sergeant to speak up with more fervent details.

"I just want you to know that I appreciated meeting you on the beach yesterday and the kind words you shared with me." After setting down her coffee, she stands behind the sergeant to glance at the newspaper and then begins to place her hands on him. She gently massages his shoulders. Baldwin can't believe it. The woman is really in love with him, or so it seems, for devious purposes.

Walter comments nonchalantly, "Oh you did appreciate my words? How nice. I meant every one of them." He turns the page in the newspaper. "Yes I did. I had one brief moment to forget this dreadful war. You know, could we meet again later today? I'd like that. I want you to make me laugh this time."

After seeing that the operations center is completely vacant, with the scan of her devilish eyes, the attractive woman gently unbuttons one button of her blouse, exposing more of her bra and breasts. Fanning herself with her hands, she comments, "Is it hot in here, or is it me?" The headhunter necklace is clearly visible. She gently rests her chest against the back of Baldwin's head. He just can't believe the treatment he is receiving. "Oh please Walter.... You can tell me. A rescue is being planned eh?" He turns around in his chair to the view the voluptuous woman standing before him. He remarks, "Yes one is, with lightning surprise, quite, daring actually. But let's see how things go. I'm not supposed to spill the beans you know." Her warm lips move closer as she stoops over and kisses him on the lips. It is the deadly truth serum. It is too much for the poor innocent sergeant major.

She whispers into his ear, "You know Walter, I look forward to the beach. You get me so excited. I fancy you quiet types. A real man of action, a cavalier of sorts." She massages his back rigorously and mouths a few kisses along the man's neck. His blood is boiling over.

"Oh Carol," as he clutches her waist with his hands. "You play against the rules every time...You cheat!" The sergeant then gently plays with the headhunter necklace with his fingertips as it dangles before him. "The general believes that U.S. Navy is sending a small attack force. The ships and planes are probably en route as we speak. You know how these Yanks are? Shoot first and ask questions later."

Carol remarks, "Quite so."

Baldwin continues, "This baron and the Germans won't have a chance when they storm that island later today. Franklin Roosevelt's Rough Riders are on their way!" Loxley smiles and gives him another kiss on the forehead.

"Walter you are such a sweetheart...You just can't hide anything from me can you, see you at the beach." She then stands up, buttons her blouse, and walks away, blowing a kiss behind her. The devil himself will soon have the information.

Walter quietly comments, "Nothing like losing oneself in one's work!" and calmly resumes drinking his coffee and turns the page on his newspaper. He is greeted by two other colleagues in the break room. One mentions that he has a meeting with the general in a few minutes. The sergeant major gathers his things and quickly exits.

The Assault Force

On board the cruiser, the U.S.S. St. Louis, serving with Admiral Halsey's Task Force 38 in the South Pacific, a detachment of elite marine forces is gathered for a sudden intelligence briefing. The marine unit, attached to the Third Marine Division, has been resting after a series of successful "hit and run" raids on Japanese forces in the Solomon Islands. They have received another call of duty to assault the baron's island.

Leading the attack will be Boise, Idaho native Captain Harold Kirkpatrick, who is the right man for the job, having chalked up previous experience in the Guadalcanal and the Solomon Islands. He is seated in the small staff room along with his 30-man strong brigade. A marine and navy officer enter the room as it is called to attention. All of the men stand, until "At ease!" is issued. The cruiser is part of a small, rapid deployment flotilla of sorts, tasked with a very special mission.

Rear Admiral Burroughs begins his briefing to the combat-ready soldiers seated before him, along with his adjutant, helping him with the board and easel. "Men, you have been called in today to be briefed on a special operation deep inside the maritime territory of Japan. This operation is of the highest priority, but unfortunately, details of the target area are… sketchy at best. What is hampering us is that for some strange reason, no aerial photographs of this island exist. Not in our folders, the Air Corps, or those with the R.A.F. Imagine that!" Some of the marines snicker among themselves with the touch of humor of the admiral's last statement, indicating bureaucratic bungling.

Captain Kirkpatrick enters the discussion. "Commander Burroughs, Sir. Let me guess, what you are telling us is that we are about to go in and take a Phantom Island (Some of his men snicker once again) without any maps but based on some handwritten notes and crude sketches?"

The navy officer glances at his colleague at the map easel, shares a nod of the head of acknowledgement to the captain's statement, and replies with humor, "How did you know that Captain? Would you like to join G-2 Intelligence? They are looking for a few good men." Laughter fills the room. "Anyway, you make a good spy. Better yet, you ought to give this briefing..." There is more laughter as the officer points his papers toward Kirkpatrick from the podium.

"Now, one week ago, a B-25 bomber with the Tiger Squadron on Port Moresby was on a routine attack against a Japanese convoy headed for Empress Augusta Bay. Now, during that raid the aircraft was blown way off course during the nasty typhoon that made a lot of us puke over the side." There is grumbling among the men, who didn't forget the high swells. "Major, if you would please." The adjutant uncovers the first map to the combat team. The men are silent and lean forward with great interest.

"Now here is where we believe the aircraft went down, on this red "X" here. How do we know this? Well. One of the B-25 crewman managed to send out a distress signal. Through radio triangulation, based on those listening in, we calculated the crash site to this area."

Captain Kirkpatrick comments, "Sir, we lose aircraft to the Japs every day in the ocean. What makes this Mitchell so special? I mean..."

Burroughs take a deep breath and replies, "I will get to that. This raid is based on handwritten notes, sketches from a crewman from that bomber, pulled out of the water early yesterday by one of our subs. Major." He points at the easel for the next page to be shown. "Based on his sketch, this is what the island target looks like."

The island is fairly good-sized, a volcanic atoll, roughly six miles long and about a mile wide, near Nauru Island. This isn't an innocent chunk of rock, fellas. Apparently the Japanese and Nazis have established…" There is now commotion in the room with a brief mention of the Germans. "…a radio transmission station with broadcasting range of thousands of miles."

One marine blurts out "On shortwave radio? If they used that, any old smuck could pick up the broadcast from Adolf Hitler in Berlin! After all, we picked up the B-25 distress call, didn't they?"

Another soldier commented, "He's right, Sir. We hear Tokyo Rose every day. I am sure she will be talking about us and this raid quite soon. She seems to know everything,"

The commander is taken aback by the keen questioning. He replies, "This radio must be of new technology, a different range of megacycles that we cannot detect. The rescued B-25 crewman said that the Axis can use this device to speak to their subs directly over long distances. Underwater…seawater, not open air gentlemen. That is why it is imperative that we assault this island, capture the radio station, and its technicians intact."

Kirkpatrick interjects, "And rescue the aircrew."

The navy commander pauses, then says, "Of course, to save the aircrew, if they are still alive." It is becoming obvious that the lives of the aircrew are not the top priority. Burroughs continues. "The Office of Naval Intelligence is extremely interested in this secret German project. So I am asking you guys, don't go in all guns blazing. Beware of westerners in civilian clothes, or German navy personnel, they are the brains of the whole outfit. Which reminds me, there is another individual on the island of interest, a Dutchman of noble background named Carl Vandermeer, who is running an opium smuggling operation. He is to be captured alive if possible."

The briefing continues. "From what we have learned, from the debriefing by the crewman of the B-25, *Bugs Bunny* is that…" The marines in the room react as Captain Kirkpatrick stops the navy officer mid-sentence. "Hold on! Sir…What did you say?" The room is now silent.

"Did I hear you correctly? *Bugs Bunny?*

The navy officer replies, "Yes, *Bugs Bunny,* the name of the missing aircraft."

The marine captain answers back, "Oh well, I guess this raid could be a hare-raising ordeal. Maybe risky for me and my men." There is mild laughter. "The Germans are well known for very tight security. I doubt that they would leave such a secret device relatively unprotected. This is again, based on a plotted radio message and a few notes scribbled on a piece of paper. It tends to make us a bit nervous. Added to it, there are *no* aerial photographs in existence. Commander, if we find this island and then storm it, what are the disposition of enemy forces waiting for us? Where do we hit the beach?"

Rear Admiral Burroughs flips over the next paper on his podium. He replies, "I was just going to brief you on that Captain. What the Air Corps sergeant related in his report is that the enemy is comprised of a company of Japanese troops. Maybe thirty men, lightly armed, no artillery, with maybe a few woodpecker machine guns. There is a small airfield with two A6M3 Zero, Hamp fighters. It is well camouflaged. He said that he and a colleague blew up a Zero during their escape attempt from the prison cage. There is a small headquarters for the Dutchman, Japanese commander and a tent city for the Japs, local natives and Germans…"

"What about the Germans?" a soldier shouts aloud.

The officer continues. "There is a small detachment of *Waffen S.S.* (The room comes alive with commotion) tasked with guarding their radio station." The marines still discuss their formidable enemy among themselves. "Look guys, we're not talking about a division here but an estimated strength of maybe ten men in all!" There is a sigh of relief. "Also, there is a small group of Indian troops of equal number, not well equipped or trained. They are being used mostly for propaganda purposes and should not pose a serious threat."

"As for the raid, we believe that the best location to attack the island is on its eastern shore, near this dock area." Burroughs points the location on the large drawing. "This will prevent any of the enemy from escaping. After we hit that area with smoke, three Dumbo PBY's will fly your men in, and you will attack and secure the area. The remaining enemy boats will be used for the removal of the German radio equipment and technicians. Two King-fisher aircraft from our ship, the St. Louis, will provide air cover and bomb the airfield with its Zero fighters. A seaplane tender is accompanying us and will provide us with an additional four Kingfishers from the Australians. A long-range fighter may be involved as well."

"The island will be hit quickly to eliminate the enemy combat forces with several strafing runs. Rescue the remaining crewman from the *Bugs Bunny* and secure the island and then remove all German technical personnel and equipment. Handle with care men. We need to get our hands on that stuff. We are heading for the target area as we speak. Mount up and prepare for this quickie. God bless you all and good luck. I will be in the lead aircraft. We should disembark in the next four hours. We will take this island with complete surprise, and they won't know what hit them. See you on deck at noon. That is all."

The Final Option

A group of soldiers are assembled in an open field under the mid-afternoon sun. The Japanese bring forth Argendizo, who is terrible shape from solitary confinement. Major Bhavnani, and his Indian Legionnaires arrive at the site of execution. A Japanese sergeant explains to Bhavnani the reason for the injuries to the prisoner. "The American would not cooperate with the interrogation...and answer any of our questions."

Argendizo spits blood with pride. "He has sent two of my men to the field hospital. It took five soldiers just to keep this man down before he could be shackled." Two Japanese soldiers hustle the Associated Press reporter with his arms tied behind his back to a solitary post and secure him for execution. He is blindfolded. "I ain't afraid of you guys. I have my faith in my God and my country....Go ahead, pull the damn trigger!"

Baron Vandermeer is sitting at his desk engrossed in the daily routine of adjusting in his ledger book concerning his latest profits for deliveries of opium to the West. The scout car suddenly skids to a halt in front of the baron's lair. Colonel Yakashi hustles into the building in record speed. Not bad for a gentleman nearing retirement! He bursts into the baron's office. "Carl! Your agent had just sent us a message!" He hands over the letter to the Dutchman, who quickly stands up in great fear. The Japanese officer continues. "We are going to be attacked TODAY! How and at what hour is anyone's guess." Carl starts to fidget as he reads the paper in hand and stares at his desk. He sets the letter down and reaches for his WW1 souvenir bottle. The man is gripped with fright and leans up against his heavy desk.

"What kind of forces do we have at our disposal? I mean…"

The colonel pauses for a brief moment and comments, "I have a small company of men, twenty-five in all. The Germans have maybe half that. We don't have the real heavy firepower to out duel the Americans."

Carl swallows with difficulty to remark, "Colonel, what about the Indian detachment? How many?"

The officer stands with a look of dejection to reply, "Maybe six men."

The baron tries to muster some positive news. "Well, we do have the MG-42 machine guns…" Yakashi replies "With ammunition reserves of about fifteen minutes. We also have two Zero fighters, but that is nothing to fight off the swarm that could be coming in from the U.S. Navy." The Dutchman now reaches for a pack of cigarettes. The colonel continues, "I will get with Admiral Brand and Major Bhavnani to see what kind of defenses we can raise."

Carl interjects with desperation, "The natives may not fight for us. Ask them. Any who refuse…shoot them, understood? Based on the message from our agent, The Raven, we don't have much time." Carl lights his cigarette and replies, "This doesn't look good."

Colonel Yakashi heads for the door with his driver waiting outside. He turns to the baron and says, "I would suggest that you make preparations to gather your materials and paperwork and get to the dock area or stay and fight with us. You are a civilian. I can't order you to…"

The Dutchman interrupts, "Colonel, I will stand and fight to the death to defend my business if necessary." The officer nods his head, leaves the building, and walks toward his scout car.

"Fool!" he mutters to himself.

The Japanese corporal then replies, "If I had all his money, I would grab the nearest boat and head over to the next island!"

In the jungle clearing, adjacent to the site of the summary execution, Layton and his faithful copilot creep into the bushes to view the arrangement of Jerry Argendizo's impromptu firing squad. Ed and Tex Foster each carry several hand grenades, stolen from the island ammunition dump minutes earlier, without detection. The American airmen whisper their intentions as they get ready to aim the grenades at the Japanese firing squad. Just prior to the release of the first pin, the sounds of gunfire echo in the distance. All parties halt in the confusion and turn their heads toward the direction of the boat dock. Unknown to everyone present, two platoons of marines have just landed. The pilots then agree to begin their attack in the confusion and pull the grenade pins. Aircraft now appear in the skies above the island.

Major Bhavnani resumes the execution, picking up its pace, speaking to the American at a discreet distance. "Now it is customary that I ask you, do you have any last request?"

Argendizo pauses and dictates what may be the last "mental note" to his mother:

"Dear Mom,

Well it looks like this is it, the Pearly Gates are dead ahead. I failed in getting off this island, and have been recaptured by the Axis. I stand here, about to be executed, and will soon be listening to harp music. I love you, our whole family, and what a lousy way to go! Father forgive me of all my sins!"

Suddenly, without warning, the firing squad is disrupted by the appearance of two hand grenades landing before their feet. The officer yells out for everyone to take cover. Too late! Several Japanese soldiers and Indian fighters are killed in dual explosions. Lieutenant Foster then surges forward from the bushes during the developing firefight with Captain Layton to cut the newsman's ropes and free him from the post. The remaining Axis soldiers run toward their truck and are soon on their way back to the baron's compound.

All three of the survivors of the *Bugs Bunny* are reunited, with tearful adulation. Within seconds, American and Australian naval Kingfisher float planes race over the island and strafe their targets. Layton remarks above the aircraft noise, "It is about damn time somebody finally knows we are here!" Foster then comments, "Enough of the celebrations, we can do that later. Let's get the hell out of here and to the dock!"

Argendizo then says, "What a great day to be alive!" The Americans dart off towards the dock area. Foster feels his uniform breast pocket to make sure his pilot's wings are still there. He smiles to himself. The little bag of luck prevails! They run along the main path and suddenly see the shapes of men in green uniforms. Layton shouts out to his comrades, "Dive for cover! Incoming!" All the men scatter and hide beneath the dense jungle foliage. Layton draws his knife as Foster readies another hand grenade. Explosions are heard as the small island airfield has been bombed by Kingfisher aircraft. The men crouch down as infantrymen make their approach. Tex's hand reaches to pull the pin on the grenade.

"C'mon guys, let's move! We will have Kingfisher air cover for only a few minutes more. Our planes had to fly in from damn Timbuktu to…" That is all the confirmation the ex-captives needed to know. The men are American Marines!

Jerry blurts out, "Thank God you guys got here, hail Mary full of grace!" The Marines freeze in their tracks as several draw their weapons and a few get down on one knee and take aim. Jerry stands up with his hands raised while Layton and his copilot remain hidden. The newsman then walks forward with hands raised, shouting, "Don't shoot at us, we are Americans!"

The marines are relieved as their strike commander replies, "Identify yourselves! I see two more of you hiding back there!"

Captain Layton finally stands up to exclaim, "We are the lost crewman from the B-25, the *Bugs Bunny*. We crash landed here days ago. Man, thanks for getting here!" The men exchange handshakes.

"My name is Captain Kirkpatrick, with Marine Special Detachment 44." The marine officer explains. Layton can't believe his eyes that he is finally out of harm's way.

He then says, "Thank God you guys got here when you did! We were held captive on this damn island by a ruthless Dutch drug kingpin."

The officer shakes his head in acknowledgement, "Yes Captain, we know about it." Lieutenant Foster manages to get in a few words as Layton catches his breath. "Captain, there is a Japanese Colonel…Yakashi. You will find him and the Dutchman, along with a contingent of German *Waffen S.S.,* and group of Indian troops, at the compound dead ahead. Do you want me to come with you to lead the way?"

The marine officer replies, "No, that won't be necessary. You guys look to be in pretty rough shape. Sergeant Baker here, our head medic, will take you guys back to the dock area. We have an aircraft waiting."

Tex remarks with utter joy, "Looks like we are just one step closer to a sirloin steak, mashed potatoes, collard greens, and an ice-cold beer." The former captives thank the soldiers once again for their rescue from the clutches of the evil Axis. The aircrew are slowly led away, being issued foodstuff and fresh drinking water.

The marine officer then shouts to his men, "All right guys, gather around. I got the scoop, including a sketch of the area we got from an airman Sergeant Ford, which will lead us right to the enemy.

Jerry then smiles and mutters to his comrades, "Ford got through! How about that!"

There are smiles among them. However, Tex comments, "No word about Sergeant Komorowski." All the joy ends abruptly. They all assume he has perished.

Captain Kirkpatrick briefs his soldiers, holding up his diagram for all to see. "Up ahead on this road is a small airfield, and immediately behind it is a radio hut, bamboo prison stockade, field kitchen, tents, and the baron's bungalow. The German secret radio radar contraption is just north of it. Capture all technicians, got it?! Washington wants to get their hands on this equipment ASAP! Okay, A-squad and B-squad, let's fan out! On the double! Move out!" The marines quickly surge forward into the jungle as the remaining men of the *Bugs Bunny* board a PBY Catalina float plane at the dock area.

The Last Stand

Colonel Yakashi gathers his men around him in front of the baron's bungalow. A scout car stops in front of them with the Indian Legion aboard. Major Bhavnani salutes the officer. "Colonel Yakashi, the Americans have taken the dock area. I have lost several men, and they are heading in this direction."

The colonel didn't want to hear that. He looks extremely worried, "Major, how many men do you have left?"

Bhavnani replies, "Just us four." Bad news.

Yakashi looks over the area and turns to the Indian officer. "Major, I want you to set up both of your MG42's on either side of this courtyard with overlapping fields of fire. Who knows. Maybe, just maybe, we can take all of them out." The major then assists his men in getting the gun positions setup to fortify the baron's sturdy dwelling.

In the immediate vicinity, the U.S. Marines make excellent progress as they storm the airstrip with both Zero fighters ablaze, courtesy of the handiwork of U.S. naval aircraft. "The place is deserted Sir! Nobody is here!" a senior sergeant tells Kirkpatrick.

The officer then replies, "We have more jungle separating us from that compound. Tell the men to watch for booby traps."

The sergeant acknowledges, "Yes Sir! I will tell the men."

The Americans advance slowly through the dense undergrowth, and fortunately for them, two African lions are startled and run away from the men in green. The GI's exchange looks as Captain Kirkpatrick arrives. One corporal tells a colleague, "What's wrong with this picture?"

The other replies, "Beats me, but those cats are not supposed to be here, but back in Africa!"

The captain then replies, "Did you guys see that? What in the world?"

The soldier standing next to him answers, "I ain't gonna be their next lunch. This M1 Garand will see to that!"

The men surge ahead and reach a line of trees as several shots are fired at them from the compound. The colonel, baron, and the remnants of their forces hold their last-ditch defense. Several GI's run forward and are cut down by the Indian manned MG42 machine guns. The high rate of fire of the German weapon startles the attackers. "Damn it! They got two heavy MG's! Hit the dirt, stay down!" Captain Kirkpatrick shouts among his men and motions for his adjutant to come forward. "Sergeant, bring up the flame throwers. Now! We are gonna barbeque their asses!" Within minutes, two special teams armed with the flame-throwing equipment arrive at the fire fight. The two groups move ahead and attempt to outflank the enemy position. The marines provide effective cover fire.

Two *Waffen S.S.* men see the impending fire trap developing before them. One soldier shouts alarm, *"Flammenwerfer!"* and begin to pour counterfire with their Axis partners and tries to hold back the enemy. The special marine teams are pinned down. Captain Kirkpatrick surveys the desperate situation and grabs his walkie talkie. He screams at his operations chief, "This is MONGOOSE to CHIEF, come in, over!"

The radio comes to life, "Read you loud and clear!" The captain continues, "I need air support, damn it! Air support, I am marking target with smoke! Over!" One of the marines pops off two smoke grenades into the enemy positions, marking them for certain destruction. Contact is made with a lone Marine F4U Corsair fighter plane, which jettisons its external fuel tanks.

The pilot converges on the target area with great precision and dives down for his first strafing pass.

Captain Kirkpatrick shouts to his men, "Get small! Get small!" His remaining men dive for cover as the sound of the Corsair covers the battlefield. A long burst of six 50-caliber machine guns lay waste the Indian and *S.S.* men. They are torn to pieces under the cloud of dust.

The marine officer lifts his head and lets the smoke clear, as he no longer hears enemy gunfire. He then stands up and yells out, "All right men! Forward! Let's go!" The officer draws his Colt-45 pistol and leads the charge and sees nothing but death and destruction before him. Bodies are strewn everywhere. The flamethrower units spring into action, setting all the surroundings ablaze. The baron's building is dead center in their crosshairs. Several shots now ring out as Colonel Yakashi and a fellow soldier open fire with their rifles, killing two marines. Kirkpatrick manages to get cover to escape certain death. He empties another clip of ammunition in the direction of the last Japanese resistance.

The elusive Carl Vandermeer, Japanese colonel, and three other soldiers now fortify the compound. The U.S. Navy airplane again strafes the compound. Colonel Yakashi proves himself an expert marksman and manages to kill several more enemy soldiers from within Carl's building.

In back of his study, the baron sits down at his piano and proudly plays a score from Richard Wagner's tragic overture of *Die Fliegender Hollaender* (The Flying Dutchman). The sounds of explosions and gunfire fail to disrupt his last performance. It appears that death will soon be descending on our villainous narcotics baron. Suddenly he stops playing as a thought crosses his mind. He smiles deviously and begins to play a few bars of the traditional Irish melody, *"It's a Long Way to Tipperary"* and then he vanishes into a nearby closet like a phantom.

The Japanese defense in the compound continues to hold as the mysterious baron reappears from his study minutes later wearing a battered R.A.F. pilot's uniform. Yakashi and the two soldiers occupying the next room turn to take notice and are stunned at the sight. Amid the curses of the colonel, Carl draws a revolver, and remarks *"Sayonara, taihen tanoshikatta desu!"* (Good-bye, I had a delightful time) and shoots the men, killing them in cold blood. Colonel Yakashi unsuccessfully tries to get out his pistol to shoot the Dutchman and mutters his last words, "You bastard, may you burn in hell!"

The baron removes his glasses and exits the back of his building as two marine flame-throwing squads burn the entire building to the ground. The baron's desk and symbolic World War I souvenir bottle perish in the inferno.

The Flying Dutchman

Carl escapes the holocaust and runs in the direction of the bamboo stockade.
After opening the door to the pen, he throws himself to the ground and lies
motionless. American soldiers have now cleared the entire compound of the
last Japanese resistance. Several marines eventually locate the semiconscious
"British airman" and provide him with water from a canteen. He remarks in a
pure British accent, "Thank God you chaps arrived in time. They were bloody
well going to shoot me!" He exchanges handshakes after he is helped to his
feet. One GI remarks, "What happened to you? How did you get here?"

The baron replies, "My name is Warrant Officer Ronald Lambert, No. 35
Transport Squadron, R.A.F. I've been here, held up on this God-forsaken island
for months after my Dak (C-47 Dakota) was shot down. I am the only one left.

A Dutch baron who had gone crackers was going to have me shot…and
now you Yanks are here! Simply smashing!" A marine private offers Carl a
cigarette and lights it for the "pilot" as he is shepherded toward the dock area.
In the distance, one lieutenant takes Captain Kirkpatrick aside, points to Vandermeer, and remarks, "A little bit old for a pilot, wouldn't you say Harry?"

The officer then replies, "I'm not surprised. You know what England has
been through so far, Battle of Britain, North Africa… If this war drags on we'll
be doing the same thing. Even the Boy Scouts will get their draft notices!"

The baron continues his nervous, rambling discussion with several marines. "I tell you, this place is crawling with Japanese and Nazis. They were testing some kind of radio transmitter, just north of here. I tried to nobble with it you know, cut a wire here and there, so *Herr Hitler* doesn't get the message."

One marine is irritated by the monologue and comments, "Sure buddy. C'mon, keep moving. We will capture that device shortly. Washington can't wait to get their hands on it. By the way, do you know the whereabouts of this drug baron, Vandermeer?"

The baron answers, "I thought he had fled the island in a boat. Can't say I've seen him since last night. I saw him carrying two suitcases. Bloke probably escaped...Damn!" The soldiers escort him back to the dock and are eventually loaded aboard an assault boat, and he is soon aboard one of the Catalinas. Carl remains cleverly disguised in his pilfered R.A.F. uniform.

Onboard the cruiser, St. Louis, the three exhausted airmen scramble aboard the ship, which is poised off the island's coast. The remaining men of *Bugs Bunny* eventually receive a hero's welcome aboard a cruiser with its destroyer escort.

After a half-hour flight, Carl is also taken to the St. Louis. The Dutchman scales up the ropes along the side of the ship with the help of the Marines. Commander Eugene Fullerton, the ship's captain, greets him. After the salutes are exchanged, the captain invites the British airman to join him for an evening dinner in the officer's mess with the American crew. Carl Vandermeer declines, citing needed rest after the horrible ordeal of captivity. He graciously thanks the captain for the invitation, renders the proper salute, and is promptly escorted by a seaman to his private quarters. In passing, he asks the commander for the location of the bomber crew, suggesting a later visit. The uniformed baron nervously walks under escort among the crew, hoping to avoid any contact with the crew of *Bugs Bunny*. He does spot Argendizo at the ship's railing and promptly keeps his back turned and face concealed. Carl looks carefully at his uniform and realizes it has to go. He is thankfully led away and is given a private cabin and a set of U.S. Navy clothes. His ruse continues unhampered, and he conspires to murder Captain Layton at his earliest possible convenience.

Death of the Agent

General Kingston reenters the operations room to proudly announce that all of the surviving crew of *Bugs Bunny* have been rescued. "This alleged baron has yet to be located. The American soldiers on the island claim that he was killed when a building exploded or escaped the previous night by private yacht. We do also have positive confirmation from another marine detachment that an R.A.F. transport pilot was discovered." Loxley listens to the statement with a quizzical look and then sinister smile. The general then gathers his personnel together to make a special announcement: "It has come to my attention that we have detected a stray transmission, one of several as a matter of fact, emanating from this base. One was intercepted this afternoon and is currently being deciphered. Someone has also come forward, stating that they witnessed an individual making an unauthorized entry into the code room during the time of the message. This witness is currently in the custody of the military police, and I'm told that the culprit will soon be apprehended. We've had problems like this in the past (laughing to himself). The loneliness and desolation of this facility can cause anyone to foolishly contact a loved one using a private code. Please, do not enter the cryptographic section without my permission. Understood?" The group gives their acknowledgement.

General Kingston exits the room, leaving Samantha, Carol, Walter, and others behind. Walter then comes up to his sexy coworker and whispers in a joking fashion, "Really Carol... You didn't have to use a code to express how you feel about me." The sergeant major then sits down at his desk with a smile and resumes typing another report.

Lieutenant Loxley is gripped with fear as she returns to her desk, making a feeble attempt to study more aerial photographs. Her quivering hands reach for a glass of water, struggling to take a small sip. She then tells her colleagues that she's feeling ill and leaves the room. Walter is concerned. On her way out of the building she passes General Kingston's office and overhears his conversation with the military police over the phone. The general is saddened by the accusation that his star photo interpreter has been implicated. He then explodes. "She did what? What did she say? I see..." Lieutenant Loxley then runs from the building toward her quarters, obviously petrified.

General Kingston reenters the intel room accompanied by two military policemen and asks Major Clark for her whereabouts. The angry general is told of her sudden illness and remarks, "She is one sick woman indeed!" The group of men, with Walter now among them, then head for Carol's quarters. Upon reaching the officer's quarters they head for her door. An MP calls out, "Lieutenant Carol Loxley, by the order of the military police, please step outside!" There is no answer. The policeman repeats his warning and then opens the unlocked door. The group of men stand in the door's threshold and view the woman, hunched over at her desk at the other end of the room. They turn on the lights. The officials are shocked at what they find.

The sergeant major then breaks through the men and rushes forward to the desk and discovers her death by cyanide capsule. The police confirm his findings as he cuddles the woman of his admiration in his arms. Tears flow from his eyes as he runs his loving hands through her hair. The general then somberly briefs the MP's. "This officer sent the message to a certain criminal, notifying him of an American military operation in an effort to rescue a downed aircrew. A total breech of security putting the lives of everyone involved in great danger! May God have mercy on her wretched soul!" Efforts are being made to track down this criminal on the island. A contingent of

German and Japanese naval engineers has been discovered." Walter is stunned at the news and remains silent. The general then continues, "When the marines landed they found the Americans and… met a lost British pilot who… who…" (the general pauses as the puzzle finally comes together). Walter suddenly turns to look at Kingston and blurts out … "The baron!, It's the baron!" General Kingston shouts "Good God! It is! Quick! Back to the radio room! Hurry!" as the general orders an urgent message be sent to the commander of the St. Louis notifying him of a criminal masquerading as a British pilot aboard his ship.

Peril on the High Seas

After entering his quarters, the baron quickly shaves off his distinctive beard and mustache and remarks. "And the tiger quietly loses his stripes." After donning a clean navy uniform, the Dutchman then resumes his hunt for Captain Ed Layton aboard the American cruiser. After passing through several open bays of crewman bunks, he spots a large poker game in progress. In the crowded open bay he notices a Colt-45 pistol in a holster hanging from one of the bunkbed posts. The baron eases toward the bunk to gain possession of the weapon. He waits for an opportune moment. One of the seamen in the card game loses badly, claims he was cheated, and makes a scene to the jeers of the crowd. Carl exits the area, leaving an empty holster in his wake.

In the cruiser's code room, the teletype prints out the latest message. A seaman pulls the dispatch from the machine and reads the document. Another colleague, a junior officer, comes up next to him and remarks, "Anything important?"

The seaman replies, after browsing the document, "Read this!"

The officer reads it aloud. "Message from R.A.F. 23rd Reconnaissance Unit, Port Moresby. Urgent. Be on the lookout for criminal who boarded your vessel impersonating a lost R.A.F. pilot. Known to be dangerous, apprehend immediately." The officer places his hand on his mouth as he reads the report a second time and comments, "We have to notify the captain and security right away!"

On the cruiser, Commander Fullerton receives the message from British Intelligence, summons his MP's, and orders them to search every inch of the ship and capture the elusive baron. They locate and enter the baron's quarters. One soldier goes to the washbasin and notices a used shaver and soap residue in the sink, while the other notices the old R.A.F. uniform lying on the bed. The men frantically search every hold and bay within the ship, hampered by the increased number of crewman aboard the cruiser. No trace of the elusive Dutchman is found.

After crossing through several other bays below deck undetected, the big game hunter catches a glimpse of his prey. The target, Ed Layton, is walking toward his crew's bunks located near the hallway to the bathroom. Remaining concealed under the shadows of a stairway, the baron surveys the situation, noting all exits. Carl silently walks down an alternate aisle in the direction of the captain, brilliantly stalking his target. He grabs a *Life* Magazine from a bunk and ingeniously rolls it into a makeshift silencer. He strides down the line of bunks and watches Layton gather his towel and razor and head into the washroom several doors down. Vandermeer pauses briefly and smiles as two seamen pass before him. He is bumped accidentally and briefly struggles to keep the Colt from falling out of his right pants pocket. So far he is unnoticed and blends in well with his surroundings. The intrepid hunter has the target in sight and is in hot pursuit.

In the washroom stands a long line of sinks where Layton begins to lather his face with shaving cream. He looks into the mirror to make sure he hasn't missed a spot. Like a python snake in the tall grass, Carl slowly glides into the room behind the American pilot, closing two doors behind him. Shielded by a corner in the room, the hunter draws his weapon and steps forward. He stuffs the gun barrel into the rolled magazine, poised to strike. At that very instant, Layton's copilot enters the washroom from the toilets with a towel draped over his shoulder, notices the Dutchman, and shouts alarm. "Ed!" Layton is startled as Randy charges the baron, lunges for the weapon, and pushes Carl to the side. The gun discharges into Foster's abdomen as he crumples to the floor clutching his stomach in pain.

Layton springs forward, grabs the baron's right wrist still holding the weapon, and pins him to the wall. He batters the baron's hand against the bulkhead until the gun falls to the floor. The captain then kicks the pistol with his foot as it slides past Foster to the other end of the washroom. Several punches are exchanged as both combatants wrestle each other on the floor. They roll toward the gun, now within reach of the baron's grip. Carl straddles the pilot, grabs the 45-pistol, and aims it at Layton's head. Ed fights for dear life as his hands twist the pistol barrel away from his eyes. Carl squeezes the trigger and wildly fires twice into the walls during the ensuing fight.

Ed eventually uses his feet to pull the baron's torso backward, causing him to fire several shots into the ceiling. The last volley of shots empty the magazine. The men get on their feet as the enraged baron slams the pilot against the wall and begins to crush his throat with his left elbow. Layton is helpless and on the verge of blackout. He shouts, "Tell me, did you get just as much of a thrill hunting down and killing that whole R.A.F. crew! Bastard!"

The baron replies, "Of course! Before you join them, have you any last requests?"

Layton shakes his head, "I'm not going to be another trophy on your wall!"

"Goodbye Captain, the pleasure was entirely mine. You were the best target I ever faced!" the baron utters as he continues to choke the last breath out of the airman. Military policemen enter the washroom after the door is pried open with their guns drawn, but they are unable to fire due to the close distance between the two combatants. Suddenly a knife is thrown across the room into Carl Vandermeer's back. Argendizo's aim proves perfect once again as the baron collapses to the floor and dies. The MPs then move forward to collect his body. Layton, Ford, and Argendizo rush to aid their stricken comrade.

Blood runs out onto the floor as Layton grabs Randy's towel and uses it to stop the bleeding. Jerry Argendizo shouts for a medic. They attempt to comfort their mortally wounded copilot. Foster regains consciousness, stares aimlessly into space, and utters, "I guess my little bag of luck has finally run out Ed…"

Layton then replies with tears forming in his eyes "Hang on Buddy, just hang on. The medics are coming. You'll be fine!" The pilot then repositions Foster to make him more comfortable on the washroom floor. Randy reaches into his pants pocket and hands his comrade his pilot wings. Their hands are folded together. Shouts are heard in the commotion outside the washroom.

"The medics are here! Coming through!" Foster remains calm amid the pain and tries to talk. "Ed," he strains with a chuckle. "Here, I won't be needing these anymore…" He musters a smile for the last time. "I'll soon be flying on… the wings…of angels…" Lieutenant Randy "Tex" Foster closes his eyes and passes away. The men weep openly as they mourn his loss. The copilot is buried at sea the next morning with full military honors.

Ceremony on Capitol Hill

The surviving members of *Bugs Bunny* are removed from the Pacific war zone and are assembled at Capitol Hill in Washington D.C. for an award ceremony weeks later. Presiding over the event in the House chamber is the honorable Henry L. Stimson, Secretary of War. Accompanying him in the decoration of the aircrew is Army Air Corps Commander-in-Chief Henry H. Arnold.

The men line up before the packed chamber and are introduced to the congressman. The cameras flash and the newsreel film rolls to record the event. The Associated Press is represented by no other than Mr. Argendizo! He mans a tripod-mounted film camera with a smile of satisfaction. The Secretary addresses the nation as he steps up to the microphones.

"Mr. President, Speaker of the House, members of Congress, military and the nation, we are gathered here today to acknowledge the daring exploits of a bomber crew, the men of the B-25 265217 *Bugs Bunny* assigned to the 823rd bombing group on New Guinea. These brave men have gone well above and beyond the call of duty in the service of their country during this perilous war against the Axis Empire. Almighty God, let these men serve as an inspiration to our nation's efforts to restore peace and prosperity to our troubled world. Joining me in the Congressional Chamber this afternoon is our army air corp. Commander General Henry H. Arnold."

The top military brass and the bomber crew stand before the Congress bathed in the light of flash bulbs and news film cameras. Secretary of War Stimson continues his address:

"During their tour of duty with the 823rd, Captain Layton's crew has amassed a total of forty-two successful missions against the enemy, sending ten ships to the bottom of the South Pacific, including two Japanese destroyers. It is men of this caliber and dedication that are being decorated here this afternoon. On August 19, 1943, the crew was posted missing in action during an attack on a heavily armed convoy between the island of New Britain and Bougainville. Upon their rescue on the 21st of August, these men assisted in the discovery and capture of a new secret German weapon. Our forces have recovered the device this past week intact, along with its engineers and technical personnel. I am not obliged at this moment to shed any specific details. However, I will add that it is of major strategic importance.

On behalf of President Franklin Delano Roosevelt, Vice President Henry Wallace, and myself, we honor your exemplary military service to this nation with the presentation of the Distinguished Flying Cross. I will introduce each man, as General Arnold will make the individual presentations. Please hold your applause until the last award is given." General Arnold moves toward the first airman on the floor for the presentation.

"Pilot, Captain Edward Russell Layton, Waupaca, Wisconsin."

Captain Layton and General "Hap" Arnold salute each other. The general pins the medal on him as the cameras click in the chamber, and he remarks "Captain, please accept this award of the Distinguished Flying Cross for your fine service and dedication to the United States Army Air Corps." His wife gleams with joy. A handshake is given, certificate issued, and then a final salute is rendered. "Thank you Sir!" the captain answers solemnly.

"Copilot, Lieutenant Randall Howard Foster, Abilene, Texas."

General Arnold steps forward to the widow and family of the fallen airman. "Mrs. Foster, and family, I join you in mourning the loss of your husband. He was an outstanding airman, and we are very proud of his service to this country and the United States Army Air Corps. Please accept this posthumous award of the distinguished Flying Cross." He hands the widow a case containing the medal and certificate. Tears flow among the entire family. "Please accept my heartfelt condolences." The remaining crewmen also are fighting back the tears.

"Staff Sergeant Charles T. Wozniak. Cleveland, Ohio."

The Air Force general steps forward to greet the family of Staff Sergeant Charles T Wozniak, from Cleveland, Ohio, the B-25 tail gunner who perished off the coast of the mysterious island.

The general remarks, "Mr. and Mrs. Wozniak, please accept this decoration of the Distinguished Flying Cross for your son's exemplary service in the United States Army Air Corps. Please accept my heartfelt condolences and our hearts and prayers go with all of you during this most difficult time."

"Staff Sergeant Daryl Ford, Rapid City, South Dakota."

General Arnold steps forward to the Native American as salutes are rendered. "Sergeant, please accept this decoration of the Distinguished Flying Cross for your fine service in the United States Army Air Corps." Salutes are exchanged. The general remarks, "Nice to see you back in the right uniform Son," The officer pats him on the shoulder with a big smile. Sergeant Ford responds solemnly, "Yes Sir!" and manages a smile. Ford's whole family is elated with the presentation of the prestigious award.

The group of men move toward the parents of deceased waist gunner George Komorowski.

"Staff Sergeant George Stanislaw Komorowski, Chicago, Illinois."

The accompanying officer quietly tells the general that Mrs. Komorowski understands very little English. The general stands before the parents of the deceased. The general speaks slowly as Mr. Komorowski translates for his wife. "Mr. and Mrs. Komorowski...on behalf of the President of the United States and the U.S. Army Air Corps... please accept this posthumous decoration of the distinguished Flying Cross for your son who died in the service of his country." The tears flow from both eyes of the parents and neighboring Daryl Ford as the medal in its case is presented. The general remarks, "I am terribly sorry." Mrs. Komorowski tells the general in Polish, *"Dzien kuje bardzo!"* (Thank you very much), then in broken English replies, "Thank you." Mrs. Komorowski begins to cry as she cradles the medal in her arms, speaking quietly in Polish. Her husband tries his best to comfort her.

The members of Congress then rise up from their seats and issue a re-sounding applause. The surviving aircrew gather together under a sea of flash-bulbs and motion picture film and congratulates one another. Henry Stimson quiets the crowd as the members take their seats in the chamber. General Arnold steps forward to the podium.

"Mr. President, Speaker of the House, Congress. My name is General Henry Arnold, commander of the United States Army Air Corps. I would like to say that the Fifth Air Force Commander General Kenney and I are proud of these men serving in this Bomb Group on New Guinea. Their commander, Colonel Ryan T. Kendall, has led his men through very bitter combat in the theatre over the last several months. As previously mentioned by the Secretary of War, the 823rd Bomb Squadron distinguished itself on August 19, 1943 during a raid on a Japanese convoy off the coast of Bougainville, inflicting heavy losses to the enemy. On behalf of President Franklin Delano Roosevelt, I wish to present the 823rd Bomb Squadron with the Presidential Unit Cita-tion, issued this day, August 28, 1943 by the president, for the unit's faithful and distinguished combat service, second to none in the South Pacific."

The *Bugs Bunny* in Combat in the South Pacific: The Real Story

During the autumn of 1944, Allied forces in the South Pacific had gained the upper hand against the once formidable Japanese Empire over the skies and waves, but their troops were bogged down in the bitter "Island Hopping' campaign. General Douglas MacArthur now aimed his forces toward the Philippines. The losses in men and equipment were considerable. necessitating the addition of more tactical air power in the continued conflict.

Flying in support of the military campaign in the Pacific Theatre were the men of the 823rd Bomb Squadron 38th Bombing Group. When they entered combat in October as part of Lieutenant General G.C. Kenney's Fifth Air Force, they were determined to put out the light of imperial Japan's rising sun. This squadron, likes its counterparts in the hostile skies of the Far East, had flown thousands of miles from its origin in Savannah, Georgia to answer the call of duty. The 823rd "Tigers" would see action over New Guinea, the Dutch East Indies, Philippines, Formosa (now Taiwan), and stretching its sphere of influence as far north as the east coast of China before the cessation of hostilities.

Amongst the rank and file of the 823rd stood 2nd Lieutenant Erwin Werhand. The farm boy from Medford, Wisconsin never dreamed of the scenes of what were to face him during the Pacific War. Drafted into the U.S. Army in July of 1941 and assigned to a medical unit supporting an infantry division, Erwin's passion for flying was stirred by a training incident at Camp Lee, Virginia. He recalled:

> "When we were hiking along on maneuvers one day, they came at us with a Lockheed Hudson bomber, and dropped sacks of flour on our heads to show us that we were not properly camouflaged. I'd rather be dropping the flour than catching it!"

In the wake of the Japanese attack on Pearl Harbor, the pilot requirements were relaxed to allow non-college educated men to attain their wings. Werhand took immediate advantage of the change in policy by passing his physical and written exam to begin ground school in Orangeburg, South Carolina. After successfully completing his primary training in the PT-17 Stearman and progressing through the AT-6 Texan at Marianna, Florida, Erwin Werhand earned his coveted —pilot's wings.

After completing another training stint in the cockpit of a Bell P-39 Aircobra, and bailing out over San Francisco Bay after his plane suffered engine trouble, he transitioned to the North American B-25 Mitchell based at Greenville, South Carolina and remarked:

> "I Liked the B-25 and was glad to get out of the fighter type aircraft. It had enough power to do what you wanted and (was) quite maneuverable. I could really fly the thing. Sometimes I would come in on the approach, cut the throttles, and swoop over our airfield like a fighter."

His assignment to the 823rd Bomb Squadron in Savannah, Georgia opened the door for the opportunity and experience in the Air Corps that the Wisconsinite never imagined. Elements of the 823rd were then flown westward cross-country to California to test their fuel consumption. Upon landing, the bombers were modified to accept the installation of an additional fuel tank in the radio compartment. The aircrews were then briefed about their forthcoming "epic" flight deep into the heart of the South Pacific—end destination, New Guinea.

The first leg of the journey took them from California to Hawaii. While the aircraft were serviced at Hickham Field, several of the airmen ventured to Pearl Harbor and viewed the charred hulk of the battleship Arizona and the overturned Oklahoma. *"When you thought of all the men still down in there, in those ships, it was just horrible. It filled you with revenge. Let's get this war over with!"*

The B-25's then set out for the seemingly endless journey passing through Christmas, Canton, and Fiji Islands to Townsville, Australia, where the aircraft received further combat modifications. While in Australia, Lieutenant Werhand and his comrades managed to get some "crew rest" and explore their new surroundings.

"When I went on R&R to Sydney, Australia, it was so much like America. We had flown a stripped-down currier B-25 named 'Fat Cat' used for crew rotations. The Australians were so thankful that we were in their country. I was in Sydney for about three weeks. The beer was good, and you could get liquor quite easily. We'd bring it back with us. The food was great, with the steak and eggs they offered us. We even had Christmas dinner with several women. It was so much like life back in the States."

The last segment of the trip consisted of being sent, minus their aircraft, to Port Moresby, New Guinea and onward to the island of Biak. In October 1944, the war in the Pacific reached its crescendo as Admiral Bill Halsey sent one of his carrier groups to bomb the Japanese airbases on Formosa and Okinawa as preparations were made to land U.S. troops in Leyte Gulf in the Philippines. Werhand's group reached Biak to begin their air operations, as the "Tigers" were reunited with their Mitchells. As General Douglas MacArthur set foot on the island of Luzon during his triumphant return to the Philippines, Erwin and his fellow pilots continued to adjust to their new surroundings.

"Our airfield was made up of tents and the living conditions were not good at all. The food we received was all dehydrated and tasted bad. Many times we'd leave the mess hall and just crack open a coconut. Things got so bad that we grabbed our Colt -45's and went hunting for Wallabies. We took Atabrine, these yellow-colored pills, to fight off malaria since we didn't have any Quinine. You could tell who was taking it since they got yellow eyeballs. There really wasn't much recreation apart from a few people playing baseball. Music was played over the loudspeakers from Armed Forces Radio. We got mail pretty often; however, it was always late.

The new pilots that arrived on Biak were assigned to combat pilots for initial combat orientation. I flew as copilot on a few missions, even playing the role of bombardier. Each squadron had about fourteen aircraft, and a group would consist of about forty-five to fifty bombers in formation. One squadron would stand down for maintenance unless it was a maximum effort.

Our briefings would normally start around dusk. However, times could change based on new information received from Fifth Air Force intelligence. All of the aircrews that were going to fly out were assembled. The Lieutenant Colonel would give us the target briefing, and then came the weather and intelligence men. Intel would tell us where to find the enemy guns and what types they were.

We'd usually get up the next morning at five o'clock after someone yelled out, "The Red Coats are coming!" After breakfast we would go out and meet the aircraft crew chief and go over the maintenance paperwork. Our fuel tanks were then topped off and all other fluids checked. The rest of my crew was then told what the target of the day was, and we all sat and sweated it out before takeoff.

I always packed my 45-pistol and toothbrush for each mission. We were flying over enemy territory so often that we had fear of being shot down. That scared the men the most, but I handled it pretty well. The last thing I wanted to do is go down and be captured. We knew what the Japanese were doing to Allied prisoners and heard about the decapitations. "Tokyo Rose" also gave us the latest propaganda over the radio and the bounties on all of our heads for $10,000 each. Luckily most of my time flying the B-25 was over water, and I never had any apprehension about capture. I felt quite safe in my aircraft."

The Fifth Air Force Mitchell's continued to provide tactical air support in the Allied drive to clear the Philippine islands of Japanese resistance. The 823rd was then deployed to the island of Morotai in the Dutch East Indies, closer to the action and within the range of enemy fighters. "Eye for an Eye" became the golden rule between skirmishes Werhand's group and the Japanese had during the night.

"During our assignment on Morotai, we got bombed by one or two Japanese aircraft every night. The Japs wanted us to keep awake. So then we went over (to) their airfields and dropped a couple of bombs on them every fifteen to twenty minutes. It was my turn one night to return the favor, and sure enough I got lost! Our airstrip did not have a radio beam to hone in on. Later the radio at the base came up, and I found my way home. Just as I touched down on the field, a Jap plane appeared and dropped a string of bombs across the center of the runway. I burned the tires and rims right of my B-25 and stopped right in the nick of time. We heard that some of our aircraft suffered light damage. Luckily this was the only time I had to face enemy aircraft. Our low-level flying protected us from interception."

The rugged bombers pressed home their attacks on Japanese shipping and enemy occupied territory. Werhand and his new faithful mount, affectionately named *Bugs Bunny*, soldiered onward into the winter of 1944. The development of effective tactics ensured the 823rd continued success—and above all, survival— during the Philippine campaign. Werhand described his daring raids on enemy troop concentrations and 'Tokyo Express' merchant convoys flying under his shadow:

"We'd try and hit the enemy from a land to sea direction during our attacks on ground targets. If I got hit, I could fly out to sea and be rescued by our submarines or Catalina flying boats off the coast. Our group would fly behind the target at about 3,000 feet, make our turn, and gain speed on the descent. Most of the time we'd "firewall" it and cross the target at a speed of over 300 mph. Our problem was the ground fire, since we flew at low altitudes. We had a camera mounted in the tail of our bomber, and it automatically took photos when actuated by the opening of the bomb bay doors.

We'd carry regular bombs, napalm, para-fragmentation, and even 5-inch rockets under our wings. The rockets were not very accurate, but when going against ships, you'd probably score a good hit.

The B-25's we flew were the J-models. Later they had to pull the side nose mounted guns outside my window because the recoil was pulling out the rivets on the nacelles! My B-25 was "Bugs Bunny" since he was in the cinema at the time. He was a very forgiving plane that didn't have a tendency to stall. I flew the Bugs Bunny for several months, and then I was rotated to other aircraft. It would be very unusual for a crew to stay with one bomber the whole time. We didn't get replacement airplanes quickly, and the ones we got had repair patches all over them. It seemed like the war in Europe had top priority over us."

With MacArthur's ground forces making successful penetrations on the island of Luzon in their drive to capture Manila, U.S. carrier and Fifth Air Force aircraft battered the Japanese-held Clark Air Force Base. In desperation, the Japanese Air Force stepped up the pace of their kamikaze attacks on the U.S. fleet, with encouraging results. However, their losses in men and aircraft made them less of a threat over the islands. The 823rd continued its daily raids, unmolested by enemy fighter aircraft in February and March. Erwin's group was then based at Lingayen, after the island of Luzon fell to American forces. *Bugs Bunny* and the rest of the Mitchell's pressed home their attacks against Japanese ground forces, getting riddled with anti-aircraft fire.

"On the Philippines we'd hit enemy convoys of trucks loaded with troops. I would say that we flew lower than twenty-five feet to strafe them. Luckily the Japs didn't have many gun emplacements there. However I did get pretty shot up over Manila one afternoon after dropping a load on a target. We were flying over what I thought was friendly territory, and I saw the infantrymen moving about on the ground below. All of a sudden I got hit with a big forty millimeter shell, right between my left engine and the fuselage. Boy did I get out of that area in a hurry. Enough with the sightseeing!

One time I took Bugs Bunny on a weather reconnaissance mission over Formosa. We left Lingayen early in the morning and flew out into the South China Sea. I then spotted a coral reef with a bunch of small boats lined up around it. There must have been at least 150 civilians standing on that reef. Of course it was open hunting season on everything (human targets).

So I flew overhead and fired a short burst with my guns to show them what I had. Then I circled and waved to them from my cockpit window. I wasn't really sure who they were, for all

I know they could be ferrying supplies to the Japanese. Bugs had enough firepower to kill every person standing down there. However, I could not have lived with myself and have been very thankful that I didn't pull the trigger...because then I wouldn't have been much of a person.

There were many times when we hit the enemy troops that were out in the open and running for their lives. We strafed and killed a lot of them. You could see their bodies literally evaporate after being hit with the 50-caliber slugs."

During the remainder of the Philippine campaign, Erwin's B-25's began their air attacks against Japanese shipping, attempting to resupply their contingent of forces now trapped on Borneo. This island also provided Japanese with 40 percent of her fuel and oil supplies, and if it fell, would have severely damaged the Empire of Japan's war effort. General MacArthur had believed that the island could provide a good Pacific base for the Royal Navy and new Allied airfields, contrary to the opinions of his Allied commanders who advised caution.

With the absence in enemy air traffic, the American's accidentally provided air action of their own over the island of Luzon. The consequences were to prove fatal in two instances.

"One night a B-24 Liberator came flying over our base and every gun on Luzon and even the warships off shore were shooting at this poor guy. This was just terrifying to watch as they just kept shooting at the Liberator. I would have hated to have been part of that crew! On another day I saw two Lockheed P-38 Lightnings come down as well. The two planes came screaming downward, like during dive-bombing practice, and both pilots flew right into the ground about a mile away from us. Maybe the speed of their dive froze their controls, or they were playing a game of "chicken." Who knows."

The shipping lanes north of Borneo provided a fertile hunting ground for the intrepid "Tigers" over the next month. The B-25's flew daily in their quest to send the Japanese resupply effort to the bottom of the Pacific. Newly promoted First Lieutenant Werhand vividly recollected one of the most memorable mission he'd flown during World War Two, while flying off the coast of mainland China to knock off transport ships at their source. Everything started off perfectly until reaching the target area.

"We left on a routine mission looking for shipping off the coast of China. The Japanese were shipping out from Borneo, and we had to find the ships without intelligence reports. We found three ships that day, with two destroyer escorts and one transport among them. I led this flight with six B-25's and assigned two aircraft to each target. We were at about 3,000 feet and circled the ships out of the range of their AA guns. Shipping was the worst target of all since there wasn't anything to hide behind! The enemy gunners can refine their lead on you when you make your approach. On ground attacks we'd be so low enough to hide behind trees or something else.

We went in! My target was the destroyer escort, which had been hit with the 50-caliber guns in my nose. The flight leader who was supposed to go in and hit the transport goofed up and went for my ship instead. The transport was so well-armed, and we were in a sudden crossfire. This B-25 got hit in the engine, since he was flying too high. I got hit on the left side, and I could feel it. Fortunately, I didn't lose flight control but quickly corrected with my rudder and re-trimmed the plane. We were all right. But the other guy, who flew in error, he headed inland. We did have alternate airfields in China that were believed to be in "friendly territory," but we were never quite sure. The Japs probably had overrun some of them. We could not talk with the crip-

pled bomber or stick around to see where he was going to land because of the fuel situation. We never spoke among ourselves while in formation because we don't want the Japs to hear us. We never heard from that other flight crew again. Our uniform did have the "Blood Chits" on them, to reward our captors with money and our safe return. The next day we found the remaining transport ship; I guess we sent the other two to the bottom."

While stationed on Lingayen, our pilot was treated to the friendliness—and above all, resourcefulness—of their Philippine hosts.

"During our stay on the Philippines, we paid some guys about $75 for a 20-by-20-foot beach house on stilts, right on the beach. We laid the floor down after we got some wood from the navy. The Filipinos were thankful for us being there. We had a house-boy wo would even steal chickens for us. We'd trade them out t-shirts for eggs once in a while to get something really good to eat. When we shipped out, the boy took our stove and cooking utensils. After all, we owed it him for all that he did for us."

With the onset of April 1945, American forces undertook Operation ICE-BERG, the amphibious assault on the island of Okinawa in the Ryukyu Archipelago. The Japanese continued to sacrifice their remaining pilots against the vast Allied armada in suicidal fashion. The Americans felt the bite of the kamikaze's "Divine Wind" firsthand. It was reminiscent of the typhoon that destroyed Kublai Khan's attack fleet off the coast of Japan in 1281.

The forward airfields on Formosa that provided this aerial menace over Okinawa topped General Kenny's Fifth Air Force target list, accompanied by the vital alcohol production facilities and railway terminals. Erwin's group was called into action to support the campaign, in an operation that Lieutenant Werhand earned the Purple Heart for after his cockpit was riddled by Japanese AA fire.

"Over Formosa our group was to attack the alcohol plants and airfields. The plants were top priority since the Japs had so many of them. To get these targets, we'd come in low below the smoke stacks, pop up over the stack, release the loads, and then get quickly back down on the deck again. You could see the tracer bullets coming up at you from the ground below. On this island we did see some enemy aircraft parked on their airfields. However, they were already burned out with their wing tips and tails lying on the ground. We did hit some of the remaining planes in their revetments from time to time. We flew so low on these missions that we'd discover rice in our bomb bay doors! One guy even came home with a chicken stuffed in one of his engine nacelles! We were scared, and of course we flew very low just to survive.

I believe that we were after an airfield when I got hit right in the face and in the arms with broken glass from the wind screen. I don't know if the copilot had grabbed the controls from me to help steer the B-25 for that spilt second. We were so close to the ground that it could have been fatal. Our plane skidded and hit a bamboo tree that came between the engine and our cockpit fuselage.

It is kind of funny, years later, when watching TV programs about Taiwan (Formosa), and you look and see all the tall modern buildings. When I was there during the war, there was nothing more than one-story buildings and shacks."

In the wake of the atomic bomb raids on Hiroshima and Nagasaki and the Japanese surrender to end the Second World War, Captain Werhand ventured over the mainland Japan in his aircraft to survey the destruction of these two cities, which had made headlines around the world. It provided an indelible sight, similar in intensity to his previous visit to Pearl Harbor.

"I flew over Nagasaki and Hiroshima after both bombs had been dropped. It was unbelievable to see. I mean, our B-25's were dropping bombs the size of fire crackers! I flew over each city and could not believe that one bomb had done all of that!"

After the war, Werhand was assigned as an air operations officer on Okinawa. He was the right man for the job. After all, he'd flown forty-seven successful missions without being shot down. During the escalation and onset of the Korean War in the 50's, Erwin flew the C-54 transport aircraft to evacuate the casualties. The most interesting job he had while being a member of the United States Air Force was flights northward to the ice cap in Greenland in the durable C-47 Skytrain. He provided humanitarian aid to mountain climbers, dig teams, and Eskimo villagers.

With the dawn of the Jet Age, Major Erwin Werhand cross-trained into Strategic Air Command's Boeing B-47 Stratojet, tasked to deliver an 18-megaton bomb in the event of Soviet aggression. He remained on alert status at Whiteman AFB, Missouri until his retirement in 1961 as the rank of colonel. He had relocated to Charlotte, North Carolina with his adoring wife and served as an active member of the local Carolinas Aviation Historical Commission, an organization which still fosters the history and traditions of military aviation, focused on those who laid down their lives to preserve the liberties and freedoms of the United States. He passed away in 2002 after losing his final battle against cancer. Werhand was buried in Arlington National Cemetery with full military honors.

The business end of the B-25 Mitchell 'Bugs Bunny,' bristling with eight .50 caliber machine guns. This gunship platform wreaked havoc on Japanese shipping during the war in the Pacific. (Author's Collection)

A close-up of the distinctive nose art of the 'Bugs Bunny' with a proud member of the ground crew posing in the foreground. (Author's Collection)

A B-25 Mitchell demonstrates the art of low-level skip bombing for the camera. (ww2db.com)

This remarkable photograph shows the B-25 gunships in action, while stalking a Japanese destroyer, at a perilously low altitude. The sheer heroism and guts required for this method of attack is beyond description. Amazing at it may seem, the lumbering B-17 bomber was even pressed into this dangerous, yet effective role in the Pacific as well. (ww2db.com)

The B-25's of the 'Tigers' are shown in formation, ready for their next appointment with the Japanese. (Werhand Collection)

The 823rd gunships are shown in action, in 1944 attacking enemy shipping off the coast of Formosa (Taiwan), as photographed by the automatic rearward facing cameras on Bugs Bunny. (Werhand Collection)

Captain Erwin Werhand (top row, far left) and his crew proudly pose for a photograph with the 'Tigers' Squadron while based in Lingayen in the Philippines in 1944. (Werhand Collection)

The Consolidated PBY Catalina long range flying boat. Affectionately nick-named 'Dumbo' by her aircrews after Walt Disney's cartoon character. (ww2db.com)

The terror of the skies, the dreaded Mitsubishi A6M2 Zero fighter. It proved to be a devastatingly effective combat aircraft until the advent of the U.S. Navy Grumman Hellcat in September 1943. (ww2db.com)

Bundesarchiv. Bild 1011-398-1794-18
Foto: Reiners | 1942 August - September

A German Messerschmitt 109G fighter, one similarly flown by Hauptmann Reinmann over the Baron's island, tasked with defending the German 'Merkur' ELF transmission site. (ww2db.com)

Members of the Pro-German 'Free Indian' Legion stand in formation, awaiting news of their next deployment. (Bundesarchiv)

A soldier of the dreaded Waffen S.S. carrying his formidable MG42 heavy machine gun, while in combat during World War Two. (Bundesarchiv)

The Chance-Vought F4U Corsair, as shown at remote airstrip in the South Pacific islands. This legendary fighter plane ironically ended its combat career in July 1969, during the 'Soccer War' between Honduras and El Salvador, triggered by a bitterly-contested 1970 FIFA World Cup qualifying match. (ww2db.com)

The U.S. Navy Vought OS2U Kingfisher float plane. This rugged aircraft is being hoisted off a warship in preparation for the impending raid on the Baron's Island. (ww2db.com)

The U.S. Navy cruiser (CL-49) U.S.S. ST. LOUIS embarks on another mission deep into the South Pacific. She was later sold by the United States to Brazil, and renamed the Almirante Tamandaré. She was eventually decommissioned and sold to Taiwan for scrap. She sank while under tow off the coast of Cape of Good Hope in Africa in 1980. (ww2db.com)

CPSIA information can be obtained
at www.ICGtesting.com
Printed in the USA
LVHW081013130120
643435LV00017B/956/P